99 Proven Tips

to

Accelerate Your Masterpreneur™ Journey

Shared Wisdom from Leadership LIVE @ 8:05!

ANDREW FRAZIER, MBA, CFA

Small Business Pro University Press
NEW JERSEY

Endorsements

"The 99 tips offered by Andrew's guest experts represent invaluable guidance for any business owner seeking to grow a successful company."

Dr. Randal Pinkett
Co-founder, Chairman and CEO, BCT Partners

"Andrew, this is your best book ever!

The tips are concise enough to provide actionable steps and detailed enough to offer clear instructions. This book provides expert advice from people who have lived through nightmares. It is perfect for entrepreneurs at any stage of business."

Lorraine Ratchford
Book Editor

Weekly Livestream/Podcast

"Excellent program tonight!!"
- **Marcella Giancarelli**

"This is such a good conversation with a great perspective."
- **Christine Saunders**

"Excited to see how these insights can inspire future entrepreneurs!"
- **Farhan Akram**

"Terrific episode with the interactive engagement."
- **Steven Robinson**

"Thanks so much for the information. I've enjoyed this session."
- **Leon Grove**

"This live stream is pure value—well done, Andrew!"
- **MD. Sajib Ahmed**

Join us every Tuesday at 8pm EST for our Livestream on YouTube, LinkedIn, Facebook, Twitch, or STEM City USA. Additionally, we drop a new podcast each Thursday morning on your favorite platform.

Small Business Pro University Press
Email: info@MySBPro.com
Website: www.SBProU.com

Copyright © 2025 Andrew Frazier Jr.

All rights reserved. No part of this publication may be produced, stored in a retrieval system, or transmitted in any form or by any means, electronic, mechanical, photocopying, recording, or otherwise, without the prior written permission of the publisher or except in the case of brief quotations embodied in critical articles and reviews.

Cover Design and Layout: Christzel Hernandez, Ledemyr Javier
Editing: Barry Cohen, Lorraine Ratchford

Library of Congress Control Number: xxxxxxxxxx

ISBN 978-1-970129-13-7

Printed in the United States of America

Other Books by the Author

En Español...
- Desarrolla Tu Negocio Como Un Profesional: Cuanto mas sabes, mas rapido creces
- La Guía del Maestro Emprendedor: Como perfeccionar el crecimiento desde el inicio a la escalabilidad

Coming Soon...

- Learning the Language of Business: What Every Business Owner Needs to Know
- Market Like A Drug Dealer and Win More Customers
- P.R.A.Y. for Financing: Get Your Business Financed Faster and Easier

Dedication

"I dedicate this to my mom, Brenda L. Frazier, who has encouraged me by her example to continually grow by learning from others."

Table of Contents

Dedication 6
Foreword 11
Introduction 13
Selling More 15
  Chapter 1: The Digital Gold Rush: Finding New Revenue 17
    Guest Expert - Jimmy Newson 22
  Chapter 2: Sell More - Answer Questions Before They Are Asked ... 23
    Guest Expert - Martha Krejci 27
  Chapter 3: Discover Your Gift: Harness Your Talents 28
    Guest Expert - Dr. Ravi R. Iyer 33
  Chapter 4: Hiring and Managing a Sales Team 34
    Guest Expert - Liz Heiman 39
  Chapter 5: Message Right or Not at All 40
    Guest Expert - Barry Cohen 44
  Chapter 6: Leveraging Video Content to Enhance Your Brand 45
    Guest Expert - Vedant Maheshwari 50
  Chapter 7: How to Become a Better Entrepreneur 51
    Guest Expert - Wallace Santos 56
  Chapter 8: Stop Playing Small: Communicate Like a CEO 57
    Guest Expert - Marc Williams 61
  Chapter 9: The Secret to Developing a National Audience 62

Guest Expert - Sunil Bhaskaran 67

Chapter 10: Uniting People to Create Revenue Opportunities 68

Guest Expert - Dale Favors 73

Chapter 11: Coach More & Manage Less for Extraordinary Results 74

Guest Expert - Stan Gibson.. 80

Chapter 12: Increase Revenue With Strategic Partnerships............. 81

Guest Expert - Victor M. Nichols.. 86

Chapter 13: Prospecting Like A Pro 88

Guest Expert - Stan Robinson 93

Chapter 14: 3P's for Personal and Business Success..................... 94

Guest Expert - Precious L. Williams 99

Chapter 15: Why Now Is A Great Time To Be Your Own Boss 100

Guest Expert - Melinda Emerson.. 105

Maximizing Profit.. 106

Chapter 16: Business is a Team Sport... 108

Guest Expert - Mel Solomon 112

Chapter 17: Scaling Your Business in 2025 113

Guest Expert - Clevonne St. Hillaire 120

Chapter 18: Double Your Close Rate Will Multiply Your Profit........ 121

Guest Expert - Doug C. Brown 125

Chapter 19: Outsourcing to Save Time & Make More Money......... 126

Guest Expert - Gene Bohensky... 131

Chapter 20: How To Boost Profit with Operational Excellence 132

Guest Expert - Josh Tan... 136

Chapter 21: Strategies for Well-being and Effective Leadership..... 137

Guest Expert - Vanessa Zamy.. 142

Chapter 22: Financial Management Triage for Entrepreneurs 143

    Guest Expert - Jeneen Perkins 149

Chapter 23: 3 Things That Can Improve Your Risk Profile 150

    Guest Expert - Paul Paray 157

Chapter 24: The Top Financial Mistakes Entrepreneurs Make 158

    Special Guest - Perry Nunes 163

Chapter 25: Protect Your Assets with Copyrights & Patents 164

    Guest Expert - Benjamin Dach, Ph.D., J.D. 170

Chapter 26: The Greatest Risk to You and Your Business 171

    Guest Expert - Julwel Kenney, Ph.D 176

Chapter 27: How To Make a Sustainable Business Model 177

    Guest Expert - Terry Trayvick 182

Financing Growth 183

    Chapter 28: How to Finance Your Contracts 185

    Guest Expert - Ervin Hughes Jr. 191

    Chapter 29: Secrets to Successfully Buy or Sell a Business 192

    Guest Expert - Richard Parker 197

    Chapter 30: The Secret to Raising Capital for an Acquisition 198

    Guest Expert - Kevin Bibelhausen 202

    Chapter 31: Growth and Profit: Solving the Capacity Conundrum .. 203

    Guest Expert - Scott Springer 207

    Chapter 32: Getting Venture Financing for a Venture 208

    Guest Expert - Calvin Reed 212

    Chapter 33: Secrets to Raising Capital in Any Environment 213

    Guest Expert - Dr. Randal Pinkett 219

Conclusion 220

Author Bio 221
Business Tips 223
    Revenue Generation Tips 224
    Profit Maximization Tips 228
    Capital Acquisition Tips 232
Guest Expert Books 234
Websites 237
Social Media 238
Small Business Like A Pro 239
Small Business Pro University 240
Resources and Initiatives 241
Special Offer 242
Stop Guessing. Start Growing. 243

Foreword

I first met Andrew Frazier in college through the National Society of Black Engineers (NSBE), where we both held leadership roles, showcasing our mutual passion for making a positive impact. I reconnected with him much later in life, after we both had transitioned from engineering to becoming business and entrepreneurship professionals.

While Andrew began his career serving as a Naval Officer before working as a corporate executive, his next act proved even more successful. He has helped more than 1,000 entrepreneurs elevate their game through a variety of carefully crafted business learning experiences. Andrew is selfless and has generously given of his time, talent, treasure, and touch to assist others.

This book reflects one of Andrew's most impressive gifts – his ability to not only see talent in others and draw it out, but also to help maximize its impact by disseminating it to the broadest possible audience. The 99 tips offered by his guest experts represent invaluable guidance for any business owner seeking to grow a successful company.

I am honored to be featured in this book along with many local, regional, national, and international business thought leaders who collectively represent almost 800 years of experience across multiple industries and disciplines. The way Andrew breaks down business into three key areas – Selling More, Maximizing Profit, and Financing Growth – is simple yet powerful.

As a business owner for over 30 years, I can say with full confidence that the 99 proven tips represent extraordinarily valuable insights. I am excited for how this collection of shared wisdom from Leadership LIVE @8:05! will empower you to do what entrepreneurs do best: seek opportunities, see opportunities, and seize opportunities.

Dr. Randal Pinkett
Co-founder, Chairman and CEO, BCT Partners
Entrepreneur & Business Leader
Diversity, Equity & Inclusion Subject Matter Expert
Technology & Data Innovator
Media Personality, Speaker, and Award-Winning Author
Former Scholar-Athlete
Humanitarian

Introduction

Welcome to 99 Proven Tips to Accelerate Your Masterpreneur™ Journey: Shared Wisdom from Leadership LIVE @8:05!

Building a business is a journey: exciting, unpredictable, challenging, and deeply rewarding. No matter how talented, driven, or passionate you are, success doesn't happen alone. It comes from learning, adapting, and most importantly, listening to those who have already walked the path.

I had the privilege of interviewing over 250 entrepreneurs, financial experts, marketers, coaches, consultants, and business leaders on my weekly Livestream/Podcast over the past 5 years. Each of them shared hard-earned insights, not from textbooks, but from real-world experience. After every conversation, I asked a simple yet powerful question:

- "What are the top three lessons you would share with entrepreneurs who want to succeed?"

This book is the result of those answers.

Inside, you'll find 99 business tips, three from each of 33 guest experts, carefully selected and organized to offer practical guidance across all aspects of business. Whether you're managing your finances, building your brand, growing your team, or dealing with setbacks, these tips are designed to be actionable, relatable, and timeless.

You won't encounter jargon or empty inspiration here. Instead, you'll receive clear, straightforward advice, the kind of wisdom that can save you years of mistakes and help you move forward more quickly and intelligently.

Each chapter features a business expert, their top three tips from the show, and an AI-generated example scenario to illustrate these tips. You can read the book straight through or jump to the topics most relevant to you today. Keep it on your desk, in your bag, or anywhere you go for moments when you need clarity, encouragement, or a spark of new thinking.

I hope this book becomes a trusted resource for you, serving as a mentor in print as you build the business and life you envision.

Let's get started.

Section #1

Selling More

"Your Most Important Job as a Business Owner" is the key theme in chapter 2 of my first book, Running Your Small Business Like A Pro. That's right, S&M, not the one you may think, but Sales and Marketing. If you have no sales, you have no business.

A key learning from my experience working one-on-one with over 1,000 business owners is that most of their challenges could be overcome by just selling more. Unfortunately, when it comes to Sales and Marketing, many business owners don't…
- Realize how important it is
- Like selling or desire to sell
- Understand marketing and how it differs from selling
- Know how to do it well

- Employ the appropriate amount of time and energy
- Invest enough or have an adequate marketing budget

Marketing education, strategies, and best practices are generally focused on larger businesses. Most often, small businesses should be marketing in the opposite way.

Fortunately, the experts in this book have proven methods and significant experience with small business-centric marketing. That's what makes this section so valuable and relevant for you.

Chapter 1: The Digital Gold Rush: Finding New Revenue

Guest Expert: Jimmy Newson

"Your vision is the gold map; your best product is the gold."
— Jimmy Newson

In a world increasingly driven by digital transformation, entrepreneurs must think strategically about how to innovate and generate new revenue streams.

Jimmy Newson lays out a clear path for tapping into the digital gold rush, focusing on vision, value, and viable digital products. His approach enables business owners to identify their most profitable opportunities and transform them into scalable digital assets.

Tip #1

Start with a Clear Vision

According to Jimmy, everything begins with a crystal-clear vision. Where is your company going? What do you want to achieve? Without a defined destination, it's impossible to navigate toward digital success. He emphasizes that a strong vision informs every subsequent decision, ensuring you're building something that aligns with your goals.

Tip #2

Define the Right Product

Once the vision is set, the next step is identifying the right product. Jimmy advises against digitizing everything; not every offering is suited for digital transformation.

Instead, find the product or service that already delivers proven value and has momentum behind it. This focus allows you to capitalize on existing strengths rather than forcing something new and untested into the market.

Tip # 3

Create a Scalable Digital Asset

Finally, Jimmy encourages entrepreneurs to think about scalability. Find a product that already commands your time and attention, then identify a smaller, high-value component that can become a digital Minimum Viable Product (MVP = prototype).

This MVP should be something that can be scaled easily, ideally with minimal ongoing effort from you personally. By doing so, you unlock a digital revenue stream that can grow with or without your direct involvement.

Example

From Idea to Impact: One Entrepreneur's Digital Leap

A few years ago, a health and wellness consultant found herself hitting a ceiling. Her one-on-one coaching sessions were booked solid, her clients loved her, and demand was growing, but her income and time were maxed out. She knew she needed to scale but wasn't sure how to do it without losing the personal touch that made her services so effective.

That's when she was introduced to **Tip #1: Start with a Clear Vision.** She stepped back from the daily grind and took time to ask herself the big questions: Where am I going? What impact do I want to have? Through this process, she uncovered her deeper goal, not just to help individuals feel better, but to equip thousands of people to take control of their health through accessible, proven strategies. That vision became her compass, guiding every decision that followed.

With clarity came focus, and she moved on to **Tip #2: Define the Right Product.** Instead of trying to digitize her entire coaching program, she examined what was already working well. One element consistently stood out: her 30-day detox challenge. It had a clear structure, delivered great results, and generated word-of-mouth referrals every time she ran it. Rather than reinventing the wheel, she decided to double down on this proven winner.

Next came **Tip #3: Create a Scalable Digital Asset.** She took the 30-day challenge and distilled it into a self-guided digital course, complete with video lessons, downloadable guides, and automated email support. She also added an optional group coaching tier for those who still wanted a personal connection. By building a system that could run without her constant involvement, she freed up her time while expanding her reach.

The results? Within six months, the digital version of her detox challenge was earning passive income and bringing in clients from outside her usual network. More importantly, she had created something that aligned with her vision, making wellness accessible at scale, without sacrificing quality.

Her journey highlights a critical lesson in digital transformation: you don't need to start big, and you don't need to do it all at once. With a clear vision, the right product, and a focus on scalability, even a solo entrepreneur can make a meaningful digital leap, turning their expertise into a lasting, high-impact asset.

Key Takeaways and Food for Thought

Key Takeaways from Jimmy Newson:

- Start with a clear, actionable vision for your business.
- Focus on your most profitable, high-value products when exploring digital opportunities.
- Develop scalable digital assets that don't require your constant input.

Food for Thought

- What does a clear, actionable vision for your business look like, and how will it guide your daily decisions and long-term growth?
- Which of your products or services delivers the most value and profitability, and how could you leverage digital tools to expand their impact?
- What types of digital assets could you create that would continue to generate value independently, and how would you ensure they remain effective over time?

Bio

Guest Expert - Jimmy Newson

Jimmy Newson is the founder and CEO of Moving Forward Small Business, a membership-based digital publishing company on a mission to save a million small businesses from failure by 2050, leveraging technology, innovation, and business strategy.

He is also the senior advisor for the New York Marketing Association. He presents workshops and training regularly with Start Small Think Big, NY Public Library, SCORE, Digital Marketing World Forum, DC Start-Up Week, and multiple international SaaS companies.

Chapter 2: Sell More - Answer Questions Before They Are Asked

Guest Expert: Martha Krejci

"Meet your customers at their symptoms and show up with answers before they even ask." — Martha Krejci

Martha Krejci is a leading sales and marketing strategist who teaches entrepreneurs how to outsmart the competition by anticipating what customers want and then delivering value before they even realize they need it. Her approach combines smart research, authentic content creation, and the newest AI tools to connect deeply, build trust, and accelerate sales.

Tip #1

Identify the Symptoms, Not Just the Problem

Most business owners jump straight to the solution. Martha teaches that your best prospects reside in the world of symptoms, characterized by their surface-level pains, frustrations, and questions. Start by writing down the symptoms your product or service truly solves. This puts you inside your customers' heads and helps you speak their language from the first contact, long before they ever name the real problem.

Tip #2

Use Google's "People Also Ask" to Discover Questions

Your next move is research. Martha's approach: type those symptoms into Google (not the problem, just the symptom). Scroll down to the "People Also Ask" section and pay attention to the most common and relevant questions.

These are direct insights into what your audience is actively seeking. Answering them in your content sets you apart as the go-to expert and builds instant trust by reducing buyer uncertainty.

Tip #3

Use AI as Your Content Sidekick, But Don't Copy and Paste

AI tools like ChatGPT (for content ideas) and Claude (for humanizing copy) can supercharge your workflow, but Martha cautions: don't just copy and paste.

Use ChatGPT to generate blog drafts, then run the content through Claude for a more engaging tone and personalization. Always tailor everything for your unique voice and audience. This makes your marketing feel personal, not manufactured, and keeps customers coming back for more.

Example

Tip #1: Identify the Symptoms, Not Just the Problem

Imagine you are selling business management software. Instead of only talking about "better reporting," focus on your customer's symptom: missing deadlines. You jot down as many symptom phrases as you can, like "always behind on projects" or "never sure what's due next," for use in your content and sales conversations.

Tip #2: Use Google's "People Also Ask" to Discover Questions

Next, you search "always behind on projects" on Google and review the questions in the "People Also Ask" box: "How do you keep projects on track?" "What causes missed deadlines?" You gather these real-world questions and create blog posts, videos, and resources that answer them, positioning your offer as the answer.

Tip #3: Use AI as Your Content Sidekick, But Don't Copy and Paste

You draft a 500-word article on "How to keep projects on track" using ChatGPT, prompt it with your target customer's persona, and then paste the draft into Claude with a note to match your brand's voice and make it sound more conversational. After reviewing and personalizing the content, you publish it as a blog and send it to your list, delivering exactly what prospects are searching for, in a style that builds affinity.

Questions and Key Takeaways

Key Takeaways from Martha Krejci:

- Speak first to the client's symptoms, not just their problems, for more relatable sales and marketing.
- Use Google's "People Also Ask" to learn what your audience is truly wondering about.
- Leverage AI for content but always humanize and personalize before you hit "publish."

Food for Thought

- What symptoms (not problems) are your ideal customers Googling right now?
- When was the last time you checked Google's "People Also Ask" for your main keywords?
- How can you refine your current content pipeline to ensure your brand's real voice always shines through, AI or not?

Bio

Guest Expert - Martha Krejci

Martha Krejci is an award-winning author, keynote speaker, and CEO of the Martha Krejci Company, specializing in data-driven sales automation and digital marketing strategies for business growth.

She helps entrepreneurs and organizations achieve rapid online success through systematic approaches to SEO, personal branding, and authentic automation, drawing on her experience as a former tech executive and serial entrepreneur.

Martha has been featured in major outlets such as Oprah Magazine, Fast Company, Cosmopolitan, Shape, and Huffington Post, and is recognized for empowering business owners to build lasting brands and profitable income streams from home.

Chapter 3: Discover Your Gift: Harness Your Talents

Guest Expert: Ravi R. Iyer, MD

"Your attention is your only true wealth. Master it, and you master your life." — Dr. Ravi R. Iyer

In a world full of distractions and predefined meanings, true mastery comes from reclaiming your attention. Dr. Ravi R. Iyer takes us deep into understanding how to unlock creativity, freedom, and true potential by learning to observe without judgment and allowing new realities to form.

Tip #1

Master Your Attention

According to Dr. Iyer, your attention shapes your reality. What you focus on determines the quality and direction of your life. If your attention is tied up in old stories and past experiences, you will only continue to recreate your past.

The first step to true transformation is learning to observe without immediately attaching meaning. Observation is your gateway to new possibilities.

Tip #2

Separate Observation from Meaning

From an early age, we are trained to label and categorize everything instantly, often limiting our thinking. Dr. Iyer stresses the importance of breaking this habit. Instead of rushing to define experiences, allow yourself the freedom to simply observe.

Delaying meaning-making cracks open the prison walls of your mind, giving you a glimpse into a larger world of opportunity and possibility.

Tip #3

Create Space for Freedom

Once you break open the walls of meaning, even just a crack, you unlock a powerful new freedom. With space comes the ability to explore beyond your old limitations.

You can always return to the familiar, but with the newfound ability to venture into unknown territories, discover new ideas, and grow without being trapped by your past interpretations.

Example

The Power of Perception: How One Entrepreneur Transformed by Changing Focus

After years of chasing goals and juggling responsibilities, a business coach found herself burned out and uninspired. She had all the outward signs of success: loyal clients, speaking gigs, and a growing social media following, but something was missing. Deep down, she felt stuck in a loop, repeating the same patterns despite her desire to grow. That's when she discovered a new approach to mental clarity and transformation.

It all started with **Tip #1: Master Your Attention**. She realized that her thoughts were constantly tethered to past experiences and old stories, some of which were empowering, but many of which were limiting. By learning to notice where her attention went, she gained the ability to redirect it toward what truly mattered. "My focus used to be reactive," she admitted. "Now, I choose what I give energy to, and that changes everything."

Her shift deepened with **Tip #2: Separate Observation from Meaning**. Instead of immediately assigning labels like "good," "bad," "failure," or "success," she practiced simply observing. A negative comment no longer meant she was failing. A slow month didn't mean she lacked value. By suspending judgment, she opened space to see situations for what they were, and not what she feared they meant.

Finally, she embraced **Tip #3: Create Space for Freedom**. Letting go of automatic interpretations gave her the freedom to think, feel, and act differently. She stopped defaulting to the familiar and started exploring new ideas, approaches, and business models. "It felt like I was finally breathing again," she said. "Like I had room to evolve, not just as a professional, but as a person."

Her transformation wasn't about tactics or tools; it was about mindset. By mastering her focus, questioning old assumptions, and allowing herself to just be in the moment, she found a clarity that reshaped her work and her life.

Sometimes, the most powerful breakthrough doesn't come from doing more; it comes from seeing differently.

Questions and Key Takeaways

Key Takeaways from Dr. Ravi R. Iyer:

- Gain control over your attention; it's the foundation of your reality.
- Learn to observe without rushing to apply meaning, open yourself to new possibilities.
- Once you create mental space, you unlock true freedom to grow and innovate.

Food for Thought

- What practices could help you strengthen your control over your attention, and how might that shift the way you experience your work and life?
- How might slowing down and observing without judgment reveal new opportunities or perspectives you hadn't considered before?
- What steps can you take to intentionally create more mental space, and how do you think that space could fuel your personal or professional innovation?

Bio

Guest Expert - Dr. Ravi R. Iyer

3x TEDx speaker and CEO of IR FocalPoint, Dr. Ravi Iyer, is a Harvard-trained Physician-scientist, a former Chairman of Reston Hospital, and Director of Heartland Hospice who is recognized in Who's Who in America and Who's Who in TOP Doctors of America.

Dr. Iyer is passionate about enabling the manifestation of human possibility, which is the substance of his work as a physician, in his role as CEO of a wellness supplement company, and in the educational work he does on Neuroinclusivity training and the crafting of Neuroaligned High-Performance Groups. He will be speaking today about the power of finding your gift that allows you to transcend the hamster wheel of life to achieve success.

Chapter 4: Hiring and Managing a Sales Team

Guest Expert: Liz Heiman

"Building a successful sales team isn't about fortunate accidents; it's the result of intentional hiring, clear processes and expectations, and great leadership." — Liz Heiman

Building a successful sales team isn't merely about hiring; it's about creating a strategic framework that empowers your salespeople to excel. Many businesses struggle with unpredictable revenues and a revolving door of sales talent because they lack a clear understanding of how to effectively define and manage sales roles and how to coach and lead a team to success.

Tip #1

Define the Ideal Role

Sales isn't a magical, mystical process of neuro manipulation. It's capable, caring people helping their clients solve problems. To hire the right people, it's crucial to understand the sales role you have and the skills required to succeed. Many companies rush through hiring with vague job descriptions. Instead, take the time to clarify what success looks like for each position, ensuring alignment with your company's goals

Tip #2

Know Your Sales Math

Understanding the numbers behind your sales process is critical. You must know:
- How many leads are needed to generate a sale?
- How long is your sales cycle?
- How much time does it take to manage the number of leads required?
- What payout do you need from your sales and marketing spend?
- Without a firm grasp of these metrics, businesses often overspend or fail to achieve the results they expect.

Tip #3

Manage the Investment: Support Your Salespeople

Hiring a salesperson is an investment, not just a hire. Success requires understanding what skills and traits are needed for the role, providing the right tools and training, setting realistic expectations, and consistently managing performance. Clear expectations, ongoing support, and accountability ensure that your sales team thrives, and your business grows.

Example

A CEO's Missteps in Hiring Sales Reps

I was working with a mid-sized construction manufacturing company. The CEO was ready for someone else to do sales. He believed that hiring someone who had been successful in sales in the past would guarantee success, a common misconception that led to repeated missteps.

The first hire was a charismatic salesperson who excelled at selling himself during the interview. The CEO was convinced that if this rep could sell him, he could easily sell to customers. It turned out, the rep he hired was a big talker who struggled to establish genuine connections and lacked the skills to close deals.

Next, the CEO hired a rep from a well-known corporation, assuming their success in a big company would carry over. He didn't understand the number of resources available to sales reps at larger firms, which smaller firms simply can't afford. The new hire floundered without all the perks of corporate sales organizations and ultimately decided it wasn't the right fit for him.

Finally, the CEO brought in a candidate with relevant experience in smaller companies. The rep still needed information on the ideal customer profile and effective messaging, but the CEO was unable to provide the necessary details. The CEO was expecting immediate results and fired the rep before he had time to figure things out on his own and start delivering.

The CEO came to me frustrated and looking for a better way to hire and more realistic criteria for measuring success. Once he had a clearly defined sales process, he was able to write a job description that outlined the specific skills and experience the rep would need. He created a list of questions and criteria for the interview process and adhered to them. Then, the CEO worked on creating an ideal customer profile, determining the market position, and developing value propositions. He not only hired the right person, but he also successfully managed her to success.

Setting Clear Goals and Expectations

To ensure your sales team remains focused, work from a shared understanding of what success looks like. Revenue goals should be realistic and driven by historical sales data. Additionally, emphasize the importance of building relationships with existing clients to create opportunities for upselling and foster long-lasting partnerships.

Building a Sales Culture

Creating a culture within your sales team that promotes accountability and high performance requires intention. Align the team around shared values and cultivate an environment where every member feels empowered to contribute. Recognize that sales isn't merely a numbers game; it is essential to balance activity and strategy.

Questions and Key Takeaways

Key Takeaways from Liz Heiman:

- Clearly define sales roles and responsibilities before hiring.
- Understand your sales math to avoid overspending and misaligning expectations.
- Manage the investment in your salespeople by providing the necessary support and accountability.

Food for Thought

- Reflect on your current hiring and management processes. Are you treating sales as a process that can be refined?
- Consider the patterns in hiring. Do you recognize any gaps in your current approach?
- How can you adapt your strategies to ensure that every new hire has the potential to contribute significantly to your sales goals?

Bio

Guest Expert - Liz Heiman

Liz Heiman is the mastermind behind the Re: Sales Operating System, the game-changing processes that remove chaos so companies can grow. As CEO of Regarding Sales, she helps companies build innovative, scalable strategies that align with business goals and turn unpredictable sales efforts into structured, repeatable success.

The belief that sales isn't about luck is at the core of her work. It's a process that can be taught, managed, and mastered. But the process alone isn't enough. That's why she created the Re: Sales Operating System, a framework that brings together strategy, systems, and tactics to create a fully functional, high-performing sales organization.

Liz's methods revolve around the sales funnel and the critical math behind hitting revenue goals, ensuring that every stage of the sales process is optimized for sustainable, predictable growth. When she's not consulting, speaking, or myth-busting, you'll find Liz on her island, toes in the sand, breeze in her hair.

Chapter 5: Message Right or Not at All

Guest Expert: Barry Cohen

"Benefits up front, a clear call to action, and real audience understanding; otherwise, your message misses its mark."
— *Barry Cohen*

Barry Cohen, a marketing veteran with over 40 years of experience, knows that truly effective business messaging requires more than clever words.

His formula is simple: highlight benefits, provide clear next steps, and tailor every message to fit what your audience needs most. In today's crowded marketplace, nailing these elements is the difference between buzz and oblivion.

Tip #1

Put the Benefits Front and Center

Don't make your audience guess what's in it for them. Barry urges entrepreneurs to lead all their messaging with tangible benefits. Make it the headline, the opening statement, the core reason someone should care. "Benefit, benefit, benefit, never bury it," Barry says. When your value jumps off the page or screen, you engage readers, listeners, and viewers from the first second.

Tip #2

Always Include a Clear Call to Action

Every piece of communication, from ads to emails to web pages, should make the next steps obvious. "You have to tell people exactly what you want them to do," Barry explains.

Whether it's calling, clicking, writing, scanning, or visiting in person, your CTA must be direct, visible, and unmistakable. Messages without an action point are missed marketing opportunities.

Tip # 3

Know and Understand Your Audience

Effective messages speak the language and meet the needs of the intended recipient. Barry stresses the necessity of knowing who you're targeting, what matters to them, how they view their challenges, and what motivates them to act. "Benefits and CTAs mean little if they aren't anchored in real audience understanding," Barry notes.

Example

Tip #1: Put the Benefits Front and Center

Imagine launching a new productivity app. Barry's advice: don't open with features like "integrates with your calendar", instead, headline with, "Save 5 hours every week on busywork." You place the benefit (time saved) where it belongs: front and center.

Tip #2: Always Include a Clear Call to Action

After describing benefits, you offer a direct CTA: "Start your free trial now," with a bold button or a phone number. Every social post, email, or landing page closes with this step, so prospects never wonder what to do next.

Tip #3: Know and Understand Your Audience

Before writing any copy, you profile your ideal customer: overwhelmed mid-level managers who crave work-life balance and hate tech jargon. So your language is friendly, your references relatable, and you only spotlight benefits your audience actually desires. This ensures your entire message resonates, building trust and relevance.

Questions and Key Takeaways

Key Takeaways from Barry Cohen:

- Put customer benefits in the spotlight from the very start, always.
- Make it crystal clear what action your audience should take next.
- Tailor every message to what matters most to your specific audience.

Food for Thought

- Is the primary benefit of your offer immediately visible to your audience, or is it buried beneath features?
- Does every communication you send include a clear and compelling call to action?
- How well do you really know your audience—and are you writing for their needs or for yours?

Bio

Guest Expert - Barry Cohen

Barry Cohen is an accomplished author, editor, and media strategist with over 40 years of experience in advertising and public relations.

He has helped numerous emerging brands launch successful media campaigns, spoken at trade shows nationwide, and written columns for two media trade magazines.

Barry has authored three business books, edited dozens of manuscripts, and specializes in elevating entrepreneurs and professionals through thought leadership publishing and national broadcast media.

Chapter 6: Leveraging Video Content to Enhance Your Brand

Guest Expert: Vedant Maheshwari

"Every business is a media business; it's time to own your content and drive your growth." — Vedant Maheshwari

In the rapidly evolving digital landscape, businesses that don't invest in creating and owning their own content risk falling behind. Vedant Maheshwari lays out a clear roadmap for entrepreneurs to embrace video content, especially short-form video, as a powerful tool for brand growth, lead generation, and sustainable success.

Tip #1

Every Business is Now a Media Business

Your brand can no longer rely solely on paid ads and third-party impressions. You must *own* your media: your email lists, your social channels, your online presence. Creating your own video content consistently and strategically will help you build trust, grow your audience, and ultimately drive your business forward. It's not optional in 2025 and beyond; it's essential.

Tip #2

Master Short-Form Video Content

Understanding where your customers engage is critical. Across all major platforms, short-form video has become the dominant force. Business owners must adopt a short-form video content strategy that not only garners views but also drives those viewers into a meaningful funnel, whether for generating leads, building email lists, or increasing sales. Creating frequent, relevant, and impactful short videos is now one of the fastest ways to accelerate growth.

Tip # 3

Embrace AI Tools to Stay Competitive

Artificial Intelligence isn't just a trend; it's the next big shift. Businesses that leverage AI tools for marketing, content creation, sales, and customer service will operate faster, smarter, and more cost-effectively. Start experimenting with AI now: not every tool will fit immediately, but early exploration will set you ahead of competitors who are slow to adapt. In a future dominated by AI-enhanced business operations, proactive learning will be your edge.

Example

From Overlooked to In-Demand: How Media, Video & AI Changed the Game

A small service-based business was struggling to grow despite having a solid offer and a loyal client base. Referrals had plateaued, paid ads were too expensive to maintain, and their digital presence lacked energy. They weren't failing, but they weren't scaling.

Things started to shift when the founder embraced **Tip #1: Every Business is Now a Media Business.** Instead of relying on others to promote them, they began treating their brand like a media company. They posted regularly on social media, launched a newsletter, and most importantly, started creating content that showcased their voice, values, and vision. It wasn't polished at first, but it was real, and it built trust.

Then came **Tip #2: Master Short-Form Video Content**. Once they realized how much attention short-form videos were receiving across platforms, they began recording 30- to 60-second clips, offering quick tips, insights, and behind-the-scenes moments that felt personal and helpful. Viewers didn't just watch, they clicked, commented, and followed. Video became their most powerful growth lever.

To keep pace, they turned to **Tip #3: Embrace AI Tools to Stay Competitive.** AI helped brainstorm content ideas, repurpose videos, automate outreach, and streamline marketing tasks. They weren't replacing their voice; they were amplifying it. The time they saved was reinvested into community-building, product refinement, and strategic growth.

In under a year, their inbound leads tripled. Speaking invites rolled in. Their brand, once overlooked, now stood out as a thought leader in their space. Not because they had the biggest budget, but because they owned their media, showed up consistently, and used smart tools to stay ahead.

The takeaway? In the new digital landscape, you don't need to be everywhere, but you do need to be intentional. Build your media. Share your message. Use AI to move faster. Do that, and your business won't just survive; it will lead.

Questions and Key Takeaways

Key Takeaways from Vedant Maheshwari:

- Take ownership of your brand's media and content, don't just rent attention.
- Build a robust short-form video content strategy to capture customer mindshare.
- Explore and implement AI tools now to stay ahead of the transformation curve.

Food for Thought

- How can you create and control your own media platforms to build lasting relationships with your audience rather than relying solely on borrowed channels?
- What key messages or stories could you share through short-form videos to quickly engage your audience and stay top of mind?
- Which areas of your business could benefit most from AI tools today, and how might early adoption give you a competitive advantage?

Bio

Guest Expert - Vedant Maheshwari

Mr. Vedant Maheshwari is a Co-Founder and serves as Chief Executive Officer and Board Member at Vidyo.ai, which is now Quso.ai.

Vedant comes with over 6 years of experience in video content production and optimization. Armed with an Engineering degree, he has worked with the most famous YouTubers in India and the USA, helping them grow their online presence and scale to millions of monthly views.

Chapter 7: How to Become a Better Entrepreneur

Guest Expert: Wallace Santos

"Train people to replicate excellence." — Wallace Santos

Running a business isn't just about having the skills to do the work yourself; it's about building a team and a culture that can deliver consistent excellence on a scale.

Wallace Santos, founder of Maingear Computers, shares hard-earned lessons on how to grow from being the "only one who knows how" to developing an organization that can consistently produce high-quality products and services.

Tip #1

Don't Expect Someone to Be "You"

One of the biggest mistakes entrepreneurs make is expecting employees to think and act exactly like them. Wallace candidly shares how he initially assumed that new hires would just "know" how to handle things the way he would.

But expecting someone to be "you" doesn't add up. Instead, recognize that you need to build systems and training to help employees understand how to approach problems, how to deliver value, and how to meet your standards of excellence.

Tip #2

Create Processes That Train and Empower

Building consistency means more than telling people what to do; it means creating documented, repeatable processes that guide them through each step. Wallace realized that his biggest challenge was not just hiring people but ensuring they could replicate the level of quality he himself provided.

He developed systems to train people properly, empowering them to deliver consistent results. This included everything from technical processes (like product assembly and quality checks) to customer service standards.

Tip # 3

Build a Culture of Consistency

The goal is to ensure that every product, every customer interaction, every piece of work consistently meets your standards. Wallace is proud that his team's products consistently receive great reviews, from Linus Tech Tips videos to secret shopper tests. That's no accident; it's the result of building a culture where everyone knows what excellence looks like and how to deliver it.

By investing in processes, training, and accountability, Wallace scaled his business from a small shop to a recognized brand known for quality and craftsmanship.

Example

From Frustration to Flow: How Systems Created a Scalable Business

A fast-growing company began facing a familiar problem: inconsistency. The founder, a high performer with a perfectionist streak, found it frustrating when team members didn't approach tasks the way he would. He hired talented people, but still ended up stepping in often, fixing mistakes, or redoing work himself. It wasn't sustainable.

That changed when he embraced **Tip #1: Don't Expect Someone to Be "You."** He realized his frustration wasn't about the people; it was about the lack of structure. Expecting others to read his mind or operate at his exact standards without clear direction was unrealistic. So, he shifted focus from trying to find clones of himself to creating a business that could run without his constant oversight.

That led to **Tip #2: Create Processes That Train and Empower**. He began documenting everything, from how to handle a support ticket to how to package a product properly. These weren't just checklists; they were thoughtful guides that taught team members why things mattered, not just how to do them. This transformed the training experience, empowering new hires to succeed without constant supervision.

Finally, he adopted **Tip #3: Build a Culture of Consistency**. He didn't just want employees to follow rules; he wanted them to understand the standard and take pride in meeting it. Through regular feedback, quality checks, and shared successes, consistency became an integral part of the culture. The result? Customers noticed. Reviews improved, referrals increased, and brand trust grew. Instead of scaling chaos, the business scaled excellence. Not because the team was perfect, but because the systems supported them in showing up at their best every day.

Questions and Key Takeaways

Key Takeaways from Wallace Santos:

- Don't expect employees to automatically replicate your excellence; you must train them.
- Build processes and systems that help new hires understand what quality looks like.
- Create a culture of consistency, where everyone knows how to meet (and exceed) customer expectations.

Food for Thought

- What steps can you take to clearly define and communicate your standards of excellence to your team, and how will you support them in reaching those standards?
- What processes and resources could you create to help new hires quickly grasp what quality means in your business, and how that might accelerate their growth?
- How can you build a team culture that values and consistently delivers high-quality experiences for customers, and what role does leadership play in maintaining that consistency?

Bio

Guest Expert - Wallace Santos

Wallace Santos, entrepreneur and technology enthusiast, is the CEO and co-founder of MAINGEAR, a leading high-performance PC system integrator.

Since its inception in 2002, Wallace has played a pivotal role in the company's growth and commitment to crafting exceptional custom gaming and workstation computers, earning numerous industry accolades along the way.

With his innate passion for innovation and an uncompromising dedication to quality, Wallace has positioned MAINGEAR at the forefront of the PC gaming industry, offering unparalleled performance and a unique, customer-centric experience.

As an industry veteran, he is not only an influential figure in the world of technology but also an ardent advocate for the advancement and growth of the PC gaming community.

Chapter 8: Stop Playing Small: Communicate Like a CEO

Guest Expert: Marc Williams

"You don't get better at speaking by doing it. You get better by drilling the right skills again and again." — Marc Williams

Marc Williams, an award-winning communicator and coach, believes powerful business communication is built, not born. Whether you're pitching your startup or building a global brand, you need more than talent; you need deliberate practice, expert guidance, and a vast network. In this chapter, Marc shares the three essentials that turn business owners into leaders who speak and connect like CEOs.

Tip #1

Practice Specific Skills, Not Just Speaking

You won't improve simply by talking more. Marc stresses the importance of identifying key speaking skills, like idea generation, opening strong, or storytelling, and then drilling each one repeatedly. "Speaking is built in practice, not performance," he says. Focused exercises break down communication into manageable pieces, so you master every component before stepping on stage or leading a team.

Tip #2

Surround Yourself with Real Experts

Growth accelerates when you spend time with those more skilled than you. Marc describes how much faster he advanced by seeking out professional coaches, top speakers, and networking with those already teaching, consulting, or performing at the level he aspired to reach. "Not all advice is equal. Experts raise your standard by example, feedback, and mindset," Marc insists. To communicate, and lead like a CEO, learn from the best.

Tip # 3

Grow Your Business Through Networking

No matter what the venture, connecting with others is non-negotiable. Marc credits much of his business evolution to the conversations he initiated at events, conferences, and networking meetups.

"My business would not be what it is if I hadn't started conversations with strangers," he shares. Only by talking to as many people as possible, especially those outside your usual circle, can you learn new markets, test your pitch, and unlock fresh opportunities.

Example

Tip #1: Practice Specific Skills, Not Just Speaking

Imagine preparing for a big presentation. Instead of just rehearsing full speeches, Marc recommends breaking down the process: one day, drill crafting memorable openings; another, practice concise, clear idea generation. Over weeks, these bite-sized drills made a young executive comfortable and confident on stage, far faster than endless generic practice.

Tip #2: Surround Yourself with Real Experts

Early in his journey, Marc attended a workshop led by several experienced public speaking coaches. Sitting in their sessions and even volunteering to be critiqued let him absorb expert-level feedback. This insider exposure quickly corrected years of bad habits, raising his game beyond what peer feedback alone could have done.

Tip #3: Grow Your Business Through Networking

Marc once took his business to a new level after a simple conversation at a networking event. By sharing what he did and asking questions about other attendees' work, he made connections that resulted in new clients and unexpected partnerships. Each time he practiced his business pitch or asked insightful questions in these settings, he learned and refined his leadership voice as well.

Questions and Key Takeaways

Key Takeaways from Marc Williams:

- Isolate and drill individual communication skills to build mastery.
- Seek out and learn directly from communication experts and master-level peers.
- Make consistent networking an intentional part of growing your business and influence.

Food for Thought

- Which single communication skill (idea generation, opening, storytelling, etc.) should you drill this week to see rapid improvement?
- Who are the experts in your field whose feedback could truly raise your game and how will you connect with them?
- Where and when will you practice networking intentionally to strengthen both your message and your business reach?

Bio

Guest Expert - Marc Williams

Marc Williams is a Brooklyn-based communication skills coach, keynote speaker, and co-founder of the Speaker Skills Academy, known for helping professionals and leaders become engaging and influential presenters.

As an award-winning public speaker and member of Toastmasters International, he has delivered impactful training and motivational talks at universities and organizations across the United States.

Marc holds a master's degree in education, English Literature, and Speech Communication from New York University, and is recognized for developing high-powered presentations and interviewing skills that empower clients to communicate confidently and effectively.

Chapter 9: The Secret to Developing a National Audience

Guest Expert: Sunil Bhaskaran

"Start with the end in mind, design everything backwards from your ideal offer." — Sunil Bhaskaran

Growing a national audience isn't just about reaching more people; it's about building a smart, strategic system that leads people toward your most valuable offering. This process starts by designing the journey *in reverse*, beginning with your ultimate premium service and working step-by-step backward to create a pathway that guides people to it.

Tip #1

Design Your Ideal Premium Offer First

Before doing anything else, clearly define your premium program or service, and **create a compelling title** that speaks to results.

List 4–5 key outcomes or experiences participants will get, unique and powerful enough that they *can't find them anywhere else*. This offer becomes the *anchor* for everything else you create, discovery sessions, events, and marketing funnels all exist to lead people toward this offer.

Tip #2

Create a Strategic Discovery Process

Once you know what you're offering, you can design an effective entry point, set up a **discovery session, or free consultation** specifically aimed at introducing people to your premium offer.

Shape your questions, discussions, and flow in the discovery call so they naturally lead into the premium solution. This intentional approach ensures that from the first interaction, you're leading people along a clear path.

Tip # 3

Build a Funnel That Supports the Journey

Finally, construct a system that consistently feeds into your discovery sessions, **Host webinars, Meetups, or live events** tied directly to the problems your premium offer solves.

Create vibrant communities where prospects can engage, learn, and become ready for your offer.

Ensure each step (community → event → discovery session → offer) logically flows to the next, minimizing drop-off and maximizing conversions. And remember, if someone isn't ready for your top-tier program, you can always *scale down* your offer to a smaller version, allowing them to start working with you and building trust over time.

Example

How One Coach Rebuilt Her Business by Starting at the Top

In the crowded world of coaching and consulting, many professionals find themselves stuck in a cycle of undercharging and overdelivering. That was exactly the case for one experienced coach who had built a loyal following but struggled to convert that attention into meaningful revenue.

The turning point came when she restructured her business using a top-down strategy, beginning with **Tip #1: Design Your Ideal Premium Offer First**. Instead of piecing together services reactively, she stepped back and created a flagship offer — a high-impact program built around clear, transformational outcomes. By identifying what made her work unique and packaging it into a premium experience, she instantly had a north star that clarified her messaging, value, and pricing.

With her premium offer established, she moved to **Tip #2: Create a Strategic Discovery Process**. She replaced informal chats and unstructured "free sessions" with a focused discovery conversation designed to qualify prospects and guide them toward her program. This wasn't about a hard sell; it was about asking the right questions and creating an intentional space where clients could see the gap between where they were and what the program could help them achieve.

But even a great offer and discovery process can't succeed without consistent leads. That's where **Tip #3: Build a Funnel That Supports the Journey** came into play. She began hosting regular webinars and creating community spaces that attracted the exact kind of people her program was meant for. Each step from free content to live events to consultations was connected, intentional, and aligned with her core offer.

The results spoke for themselves. Instead of chasing clients and managing scattered services, she had a clear path from visibility to value. Those not ready for her premium program were offered scaled-down options, allowing them to remain in the ecosystem while maintaining integrity and focus.

This story illustrates a key truth: real business growth often comes not from doing more, but from designing better. By starting with the premium offer, establishing a structured entry point, and creating a funnel that supports the journey, service-based entrepreneurs can transform their businesses and ultimately receive compensation commensurate with their expertise.

Questions and Key Takeaways

Key Takeaways from Sunil Bhaskaran:

- Start with a premium offer and build your process backward.
- Create discovery sessions that naturally lead into your offer.
- Build communities and systems that consistently fill your events and sessions with qualified leads.

Food for Thought

- What would your ideal premium offer look like, and how could you design your customer journey to lead naturally toward it?
- How can you structure your discovery sessions to genuinely serve potential clients while setting the stage for a seamless transition into your offer?
- What strategies could you use to build engaged communities and create systems that attract and nurture high-quality leads consistently over time?

Bio

Guest Expert - Sunil Bhaskaran

SUNIL BHASKARAN: Pronounced Soo-Nil Bus-Car-Ren is a dynamic, globally recognized speaker, trainer, educator, and author.

He brings 30+ years of building and implementing successful business plans to entrepreneurs, small business owners, and companies worldwide.

His expertise includes leadership, sales, marketing, and global business. Sunil brings a multifaceted approach to business through his knowledge of the social sciences, economics, literature, and cognitive neuroscience.

He has written three books and promotes his educational and networking events to an audience of 200,000 business owners weekly.

Sunil has degrees in both computer science and electrical engineering. He lives in the Bay Area with his lovely wife, Glenda.

Chapter 10: Uniting People to Create Revenue Opportunities

Guest Expert: Dale Favors

"Success is built on listening, adapting, and collaborating at every stage." — Dale Favors

Creating revenue opportunities isn't just about selling harder; it's about bringing people together, understanding evolving needs, and co-creating solutions that matter. Dale Favors shared that if you focus on three core practices, listening, flexibility, and collaboration, you can unlock new possibilities and deepen business relationships that last.

Tip #1

Listen Intentionally

The first and most important step is to *truly listen* to your customers, tune into their challenges, goals, and even subtle shifts in their industries.

Understand that customer needs are *dynamic*; they change over time, sometimes rapidly. Listening well positions you to anticipate changes and deliver solutions before competitors even realize the opportunity exists.

Tip #2

Stay Flexible and Agile

Business today demands flexibility.

- As customer needs evolve, your ability to *adapt quickly* determines your relevance and future success.
- Being rigid in your offers, structures, or methods can cause you to miss out on opportunities.
- Flexibility means not only adjusting your own offerings but also being willing to *pivot partnerships, resources, or strategies* to better serve your market.

Tip # 3

Collaborate Relentlessly

No one builds great outcomes alone.

- Whether it's with clients, internal teams, or strategic partners, *collaboration is key* to creating bigger wins.
- Partnering allows you to pool expertise, extend your reach, and deliver more comprehensive solutions.
  By working closely with others, both inside and outside your organization, you create an environment where innovation and new revenue streams naturally emerge.

Example

From Reactive to Responsive: Adapting Through Listening, Flexibility, and Collaboration

In a fast-moving market, a growing business noticed something troubling: its once-loyal customers were slowly drifting away. Sales plateaued, and their offerings no longer seemed to resonate. Instead of doubling down on old strategies, the team decided to take a different approach.

It began with **Tip #1: Listen Intentionally**. They set aside assumptions and started engaging directly with their clients. Through surveys, conversations, and quiet observation, they uncovered emerging challenges their customers were facing, ones no one else in the industry was addressing yet. By listening not just to words, but to trends and tone, they spotted unmet needs that opened the door to innovation.

That awareness led naturally to **Tip #2: Stay Flexible and Agile**. Rather than defending legacy systems or clinging to outdated processes, they restructured key offerings to better fit what customers need now. They shifted priorities, realigned resources, and tested new approaches in real time. This willingness to adapt quickly and without ego made them more responsive and more valuable.

But what truly accelerated their transformation was **Tip #3: Collaborate Relentlessly**. Recognizing that they couldn't evolve alone, they brought in partners with complementary strengths. They invited client feedback early in the development of new solutions and empowered internal teams to lead innovation. By embracing collaboration across all levels, they built stronger products and stronger relationships.

The result wasn't just recovery, it was reinvention. By listening deeply, staying agile, and leaning into collaboration, the business didn't just survive change. It became a leader in delivering what customers needed next.

Questions and Key Takeaways

Key Takeaways from Dale Favors:

- Listen carefully and continuously to customer needs.
- Stay flexible and ready to adapt your strategies and solutions.
- Build collaborative relationships to create greater value and new opportunities.

Food for Thought

- What systems or habits can you put in place to ensure you are consistently listening to and learning from your customers' evolving needs?
- How can you design your strategies to remain flexible, and what signs should you watch for that indicate it's time to adapt?
- How can you foster collaborative relationships that not only support mutual growth but also spark innovative opportunities neither party could achieve alone?

Bio

Guest Expert - Dale Favors

Dale is an experienced Leader, Educator, and passionate Sales Professional with a demonstrated history of managing teams in the financial services and financial technology industry. His value-add lies in bringing people and/or businesses together to create revenue opportunities.

Dale is a skilled communicator and coach with expertise in Leadership, Training, Strategy, DE&I, Asset Management, Electronic Trade Execution, Prime Brokerage, Investment Advisory, and Relationship Management. He earned a Master of Business Administration (MBA) with a focus in Finance from Florida A&M University.

Chapter 11: Coach More & Manage Less for Extraordinary Results

Guest Expert: Stan Gibson

"The best leaders are the ones who know themselves, value relationships, and invest deeply in their own growth."
— Stan Gibson

Leadership isn't just about making decisions or giving orders; it's about *coaching others through authenticity, relationships, and self-investment.* Stan Gibson's perspective focuses on building extraordinary teams and organizations by first developing the leader within.

Tip #1

Embrace Authenticity: Know Who You Are (and Who You Are Not)

Stan emphasized that leadership struggles often stem from a lack of self-awareness, not a lack of intelligence.

- Most leaders are smart enough; it's *emotional intelligence (EQ)* that separates the great from the average.
- Knowing your strengths, weaknesses, and blind spots helps you lead with authenticity.

- People will perceive you based on your actions, and those perceptions create a "reality" you must recognize and manage.

   Authentic leadership starts with stepping up to the plate and owning who you are, unapologetically and intentionally.

Tip #2

Prioritize Relationships: Build Your Personal Board of Directors

Your success and well-being are shaped by the people you surround yourself with.

- Personal and professional *relationships are vital*; they don't just help you thrive at work; they can literally extend your life.

- Research shows that *healthy relationships can increase your lifespan by up* to 60%.

- Stan advises building your own "Board of Directors", a group of trusted advisors and mentors who inspire you, challenge you, and lift you higher.

Tip # 3

Double Down on You: Invest in Your Own Health and Growth

Leaders have tremendous responsibilities across work, home, and community.

- To serve others effectively, you must *first take care of yourself.*
- Prioritize your health, emotional well-being, and ongoing development.
- Becoming the best version of yourself enables you to be a stronger, more resilient leader who can coach and uplift others every day.
- Self-care isn't selfish, it's strategic leadership.

Example

From Surface-Level Leadership to Authentic Influence: A Journey of Awareness, Relationships, and Self-Investment

In a high-pressure business environment, a leadership team was facing consistent challenges: team morale was low, turnover was rising, and progress felt stalled. The technical skills were there, and the goals were clear, but something deeper was missing.

That's when the organization began leaning into **Tip #1: Embrace Authenticity, Know Who You Are (and Who You Are Not)**. They realized that the gap wasn't in intelligence, but in emotional intelligence. Leadership began with honest self-reflection, understanding their own triggers, tendencies, and blind spots. As each leader embraced their own strengths and limitations more fully, their communication improved, their presence felt more grounded, and their teams responded with greater trust and openness.

From there, they explored **Tip #2: Prioritize Relationships, Build Your Personal Board of Directors**. No one was expected to lead alone. Team members were encouraged to form circles of support, mentorship, and peer accountability. Externally, they also sought out advisors who could offer outside perspectives, emotional balance, and fresh insight. Over time, these trusted relationships became a cornerstone of the company's resilience, creating a network of encouragement and honest feedback that helped people grow.

However, the most significant shift occurred with **Tip #3: Double Down on You, Invest in Your Own Health and Growth**. Leaders began to see that taking care of their physical, emotional, and mental well-being wasn't a luxury; it was a necessity. When self-care became part of the leadership culture, everything improved. Decision-making became clearer, energy levels rose, and people felt empowered to lead from a place of strength rather than stress.

This transformation wasn't flashy, but it was powerful. By embracing authenticity, fostering meaningful relationships, and investing in themselves, these leaders created a culture of trust, growth, and genuine influence, the kind that originates from within and radiates outward.

Questions and Key Takeaways

Key Takeaways from Stan Gibson:

- Develop deep *self-awareness* and lead authentically.
- Build strong, positive *relationships* that nurture your success and well-being.
- *Invest in yourself* consistently so you can better serve others.

Food for Thought

- What practices can help you deepen your self-awareness, and how can authentic leadership impact the people and communities you serve?
- How can you intentionally cultivate relationships that both support your personal growth and contribute to a thriving, positive environment around you?
- What areas of personal growth or skill development should you focus on to enhance your ability to create value and serve others more effectively?

Bio

Guest Expert - Stan Gibson

Stan Gibson is passionate about guiding organizations to build thriving, human-centered cultures. Through his engaging keynotes and leadership coaching, Stan equips companies with frameworks and tools to prioritize people. He advises executives on adopting transparent and collaborative leadership styles that leverage the collective wisdom of their teams.

Before founding his health and wellness consulting and coaching firm called Oxygen Plus, Stan Gibson spent 30 years in corporate real estate, most recently as Senior Vice President at Wells Fargo.

Gibson first became interested in healthy habits as a young athlete who went on to play college football at Eastern Illinois University. Understanding the science behind athleticism piqued his curiosity, leading him to discover the power of mindfulness and visualization. Gibson carried many sports philosophies into his real estate role at Wells Fargo, using the same fundamentals to breed corporate athletes conditioned to perform at the highest levels.

Chapter 12: Increase Revenue With Strategic Partnerships

Guest Expert: Victor M. Nichols

"People don't always remember when you do what you say— but they absolutely remember when you don't."
— Victor M. Nichols

Strategic partnerships can open new doors, create bigger opportunities, and dramatically increase revenue, but only if you build them the right way. Victor M. Nichols, a seasoned business strategist, shares a simple but powerful formula for creating alliances that last. His advice focuses on practical habits that entrepreneurs can apply immediately to strengthen their network and their results.

Tip #1

Listen More Than You Talk

According to Victor, the most successful partnerships begin with one thing: listening. Entrepreneurs often rush to pitch their ideas or promote themselves, but in doing so, they miss vital information. "When you listen closely," he says, "you find out what truly matters to the other person." Listening isn't passive; it's a strategic advantage. It allows you to tailor your offer, build real trust, and identify opportunities you might have overlooked.

Tip #2

Keep Your Word—Every Time

Victor emphasizes that reliability is the foundation of every great relationship. Whether the commitment is big or small, following through matters. "People may not always remember when you deliver," he explains, "but they never forget when you don't." In the world of partnerships, one broken promise can undo months, or even years, of hard work. Protect your reputation fiercely by doing exactly what you say, every single time.

Tip # 3

Embrace Failure and Keep Moving

Finally, Victor encourages entrepreneurs to rethink their relationship with failure. Innovation, he reminds us, doesn't happen without taking risks. "You're going to try things that won't work out. Don't freak out, keep moving," he advises. Strategic partnerships require creativity, flexibility, and a resilient approach. Mistakes aren't the end; they're valuable lessons that move you closer to long-term success.

Example

From Missed Connections to Meaningful Partnerships: A Lesson in Listening, Integrity, and Resilience

In the early stages of launching a new collaborative venture, a group of entrepreneurs found themselves struggling to form lasting partnerships. Meetings were frequent, conversations were enthusiastic, and ideas were abundant, but nothing seemed to stick. Promising relationships faded, deals fell through, and momentum stalled.

That's when they started practicing **Tip #1: Listen More Than You Talk**. Rather than opening with their pitch or pushing their own agenda, they shifted their approach. They started asking better questions and listening to the answers. This small but powerful change unlocked deeper insights: what partners truly needed, what they valued, and what concerns were quietly going unspoken. By listening first, they built trust and created solutions that resonated.

With that trust established, they doubled down on **Tip #2: Keep Your Word, Every Time**. No matter how minor the commitment, a follow-up email, a promised resource, or a scheduled call, they treated every promise as sacred. Their consistency earned respect, and they quickly became known as dependable collaborators. While others overpromised and underdelivered, they stood out simply by doing exactly what they said they would do.

Still, not every effort produced instant results. Ideas flopped. Timelines shifted. Not every collaboration turned into a win. But they leaned into **Tip #3: Embrace Failure and Keep Moving**.

Instead of getting discouraged, they viewed setbacks as part of the process. Every failed attempt became a source of feedback, helping them refine their strategy and strengthen their partnerships. Resilience, they discovered, was just as important as innovation.

Over time, these three simple practices, listening deeply, honoring commitments, and bouncing back from failure, transformed the way they built relationships. What began as a series of misfires evolved into a network of trusted, long-term partnerships grounded in mutual respect and shared success.

Questions and Key Takeaways

Key Takeaways from Victor M. Nichols:

- Listening is your most valuable tool for building strong, aligned partnerships.
- Your credibility is built (or broken) by whether you keep your promises.
- Failure is part of the growth process. Stay resilient and keep innovating.

Food for Thought

- How can you become a more active and empathetic listener to strengthen partnerships and ensure alignment with shared goals?
- What systems or habits can you develop to consistently deliver on your promises and maintain strong credibility with others?
- How can you reframe failure as a learning opportunity, and what strategies will help you stay resilient and motivated during setbacks?

Bio

Guest Expert - Victor M. Nichols

Victor M. Nichols is CEO/Publisher of NewarkBound Magazine and the Pleos Agency. He is an energetic and driven professional with over 30 years of proven success in strategic planning, marketing analysis, new business development, alliance partnership programs, relationship management, negotiation, consulting, and other areas. Among Vic's many achievements include the successful launches of both NewarkBound magazine and PTSD Journal; an appointment to the New Jersey Governor's Advisory Council on Tourism; orchestrating the Wine for Books collaborative program between Rutgers University and 57 Main Street Wine Company; the product launch of Imoya Brandy into the U.S. commercial market; and the design and sale of the Calicrostics custom gift line on the cable outlet Home Shopping Network. Throughout his career, he has established exceptional relationships with leading companies and notable organizations across a diverse range of industries. Representative clients included ABC Sports, Time Warner, HBO, DOL, U.S. Army, Levi Strauss, American Express, NY Jets, AT&T, New Jersey Commerce & Economic Growth Commission/Office of Travel &

Tourism, Rutgers University, Duke University, Barnabas Health, and The Newark Museum.

Chapter 13: Prospecting Like A Pro

Guest Expert: Stan Robinson

"Your prospects don't care about your product; they care about their problems." — Stan Robinson

Sales prospecting isn't just about getting attention; it's about getting attention the right way. Stan Robinson, a LinkedIn and sales strategy expert, breaks down how professionals can maximize their prospecting efforts by focusing on what truly matters to potential clients.

Tip #1

Speak the Language of Business Problems

Stan's number one rule: **focus your messaging around solving problems**. It's easy to get excited about your product or service, but buyers are only interested in how you can help them overcome a challenge or pain point.

- **Understand your target market** deeply.
- **Craft a clear, succinct message** that speaks directly to the business pain you solve.
- **Niche down** so you can become fluent in the language your specific audience speaks, making your outreach much more effective.

People buy solutions, not products, and the sharper your message, the better your results.

Tip #2

Consistency Wins in the Long Run

Consistency is the secret ingredient to successful prospecting, especially on platforms like LinkedIn.

Many prospects are what Stan calls "spectators", they watch your posts and activity silently without engaging. However, when the time comes that they need your service, it's the **consistent, trusted presence** they've seen over time that wins their attention.

Even when it feels like no one is watching, seeds grow beneath the surface. Keep showing up.

Tip # 3

Build a Strong LinkedIn Presence and Be Proactive

Finally, Stan emphasizes the importance of a **professional and solution-oriented LinkedIn profile**. It should clearly show what audience you serve, the problems you solve, how you solve these problems, and why you're the right choice.

Beyond a great profile, **proactive outreach** is key but always focus conversations on **solutions and business pain points**, not products. Build credibility first, and product discussions will happen naturally as trust develops.

Example

From Invisible to In-Demand: How Clear Messaging and Consistency Drive Business Growth

A growing consulting firm struggled to gain traction online. Despite offering a high-quality service, their outreach efforts often went unnoticed, and conversions were sporadic. After reviewing their approach, the team realized they were leading with features, not solutions, and speaking in general terms rather than directly addressing their audience's pain points.

Everything changed when they embraced **Tip #1: Speak the Language of Business Problems**. Instead of talking about what they did, they started focusing on *why* it mattered. They dug deep into the challenges their ideal clients faced and crafted messaging that spoke directly to those pain points. They simplified their pitch, narrowing their focus and tailoring their communication to resonate with a very specific audience. The shift was immediate: more engagement, more interest, and more qualified leads.

Still, results didn't happen overnight. They committed to **Tip #2: Consistency Wins in the Long Run**. Even when likes and comments were scarce, they showed up every week on LinkedIn, sharing insights, posting value-driven content, and staying top of mind. While many of their target clients never interacted publicly, they were watching. Quietly. When those prospects eventually needed help, they knew exactly who to call, the consistent, credible voice that had been in their feed all along.

The final piece was **Tip #3: Build a Strong LinkedIn Presence and Be Proactive**. They optimized their profiles to clearly communicate who they served, the problems they solved, and the outcomes they delivered. Then, they reached out, not to pitch a product, but to start conversations around shared challenges. By focusing on solutions instead of selling, they built rapport, earned trust, and saw more inbound interest than ever before.

In time, what once felt like shouting into the void became a steady stream of qualified opportunities. By speaking clearly, showing up consistently, and positioning themselves as solution-oriented experts, they turned passive visibility into active demand, proving that trust and traction are built one clear message at a time.

Questions and Key Takeaways

Key Takeaways from Stan Robinson:

- Always center your messaging around the problems you solve for your customers.
- Stay consistent with your visibility and engagement, even when results aren't immediately visible.
- Maintain a strong, professional LinkedIn presence and proactively focus your conversations on solving problems.

Food for Thought

- How can you clearly communicate the specific problems you solve for your customers in a way that feels both authentic and compelling?
- What habits or systems can you create to maintain steady visibility and engagement, even when progress feels slow or uncertain?
- How can you use LinkedIn more strategically to showcase your expertise and build conversations that highlight the solutions you offer?

Bio

Guest Expert - Stan Robinson

Stan Robinson, Jr., Chief Coaching Officer at Social Sales Link, teaches revenue-driven professionals how to create more trust-based sales conversations using LinkedIn, Sales Navigator, and AI. He has coached over 1000 sales leaders and sales professionals on social selling.

Stan has worked with clients in industries such as information technology, cybersecurity, financial services, education, law, e-commerce, business consulting, media, and government.

He is coauthor of the book Prompt Writing Made Easy: Using the CRISPY™ Framework to Leverage AI Authentically with Brynne Tillman and Bob Woods.

Stan studied Psychology at Harvard and international affairs at Princeton and continues to expand his expertise through ongoing courses on AI, sales, and business strategy. His academic background equips him with a unique blend of insight into human behavior and strategic thinking, which he applies to help businesses leverage digital tools in practical, people-centered ways. Most recently, he completed a certification in Scaling AI from the Marketing Artificial Intelligence Institute.

Chapter 14: 3P's for Personal and Business Success

Guest Expert: Precious L. Williams

"If you want to be paid top dollar, you have to show up elite."
— Precious L. Williams

In today's competitive business world, standing out isn't optional; it's essential. Precious L. Williams, the master of pitching and personal branding, breaks down her "Three P's" framework to help entrepreneurs upgrade their image, position themselves for success, and communicate their value with power. Her advice challenges business owners to elevate their game both internally and externally, and to treat their brand as a premium offering.

Tip #1

Perfect Your Packaging

Precious starts with the first impression: your packaging. "How you show up in the world, on social media and in real life, reflects the opportunities you attract," she says. From your clothing to your hairstyle to the signature elements people remember you by, everything sends a message. Entrepreneurs must ask themselves: *Is my packaging attracting the caliber of opportunities I want?* If not, it's time to rebrand your presentation to match the level of success you seek.

Tip #2

Strengthen Your Positioning

Next, Precious urges entrepreneurs to get brutally honest about how they're perceived in the marketplace. She recommends asking trusted business associates, not family, for honest feedback: Do they see you as average, mid-tier, or elite? Do they clearly understand your zone of genius? "If the feedback you receive is surface level," Precious warns, "it's time to plot twist and flip the script." Knowing your true positioning helps you refine it to stand out as a top-tier, highly valued expert.

Tip # 3

Power Up Your Pitch

Finally, Precious emphasizes the importance of how you talk about yourself and your business. A great pitch doesn't just inform, it inspires action. "Is your messaging making people want to look you up? Is it making them nibble?" she challenges. Entrepreneurs must learn to position themselves as *the only choice* that matters in their industry. Crafting a powerful, magnetic pitch is what moves the needle, drives leads, and locks in premium opportunities.

Example

From Overlooked to In-Demand: How Strategic Presence Elevates Opportunity

A talented entrepreneur had the skills, experience, and drive, but wasn't attracting the clients, collaborations, or speaking opportunities they knew they were capable of landing. Despite years of hard work, they remained stuck in a cycle of under-recognition and missed chances. The turning point came when they realized success wasn't just about what they did, it was about how they showed up.

The transformation began with **Tip #1: Perfect Your Packaging**. They took a step back and asked a hard question: Does my presence reflect the level of success I want to achieve? The answer was "not yet." From refining their wardrobe to curating a sharper digital presence, they rebranded with intention. Every detail, profile photos, content style, even their signature introduction, was elevated to signal professionalism, uniqueness, and confidence. And with that, new doors began to open.

Next came **Tip #2: Strengthen Your Positioning**. They reached out to colleagues and peers for honest feedback, not compliments. The insights were eye-opening: while many respected their work, few could articulate their niche or zone of genius. Armed with this clarity, they repositioned their messaging to highlight their unique value, owning their expertise with boldness. The shift was felt immediately, as their network began to refer them not just as "good", but as the go-to expert.

But it was **Tip #3: Power Up Your Pitch** that truly sealed the deal. Instead of rattling off a list of services, they began crafting pitches that sparked curiosity and emotional connection. They focused on storytelling, clear transformation, and a confident call to action. Their words didn't just inform, they captivated. Suddenly, the right people weren't just listening, they were reaching out.

With intentional packaging, refined positioning, and a pitch that magnetized attention, this entrepreneur went from overlooked to unforgettable. The lesson? If you want premium opportunities, you must present yourself like a premium brand, starting with how you show up, speak, and shine.

Questions and Key Takeaways

Key Takeaways from Precious L. Williams:

- Your external packaging influences the quality of opportunities you attract.
- Know how you are positioned and reposition if necessary to show up as elite.
- A compelling pitch makes you the obvious choice in a crowded marketplace.

Food for Thought

- How does the way you present your brand externally impact the type and caliber of clients, partners, or opportunities you attract?
- What strategies can businesses use to assess their current market positioning and make necessary shifts to elevate their brand perception?
- What elements make a business pitch truly stand out and resonate with your target audience in a competitive market?

Bio

Guest Expert - Precious L. Williams

Precious L. Williams is a 13-time national elevator pitch champion and the author of a #1 Best Seller for women on pitching. She has also been featured on "Shark Tank," CNN, WSJ, Forbes Magazine, Black Enterprise Magazine, Essence Magazine, and the movie "LEAP." Her current clients include Microsoft, LinkedIn, Google, eBay, and more!

Precious L. Williams is the proud Founder and CEO of Perfect Pitch Group. Top Fortune 500 companies, successful service-based entrepreneurs, and speakers HIRE her to #slayallcompetition through her powerful pitch, communication skills, and speaker training services.

Chapter 15: Why Now Is A Great Time To Be Your Own Boss

Guest Expert: Melinda Emerson

"The world is still waiting on a better mousetrap; your idea could be it." — Melinda Emerson

Known as the "SmallBizLady," Melinda Emerson has been coaching entrepreneurs for decades on how to successfully launch and grow businesses. In this chapter, she shares why the present moment is one of the best times in history to start your own business, and how both new and seasoned entrepreneurs can seize the opportunity. Her advice offers a practical path: start smart, market wisely, and never forget the customers you already have.

Tip #1

Start Smart—with Research and a Side Hustle

Melinda stresses that while opportunities abound, preparation is key. "If you have an idea that you've researched and you know who your customer is, now is the perfect time to start," she says. However, she urges aspiring entrepreneurs to start small, launching as a side hustle first. This approach lets you build experience, reduce risk, and prove your concept before going all in.

Tip #2

Create Relevant, High-Value Content

For those already in business, Melinda recommends a focus on content marketing. "Develop a great piece of content that's really relevant to your target customer," she advises. Whether it's a blog post, a short video, or an audio snippet, the goal is to position yourself as a trusted resource. Valuable content not only attracts attention but builds credibility and loyalty among your ideal audience.

Tip # 3

Nurture Your Existing Customers

Melinda reminds entrepreneurs not to overlook the goldmine they already have: their current customers. "An existing customer is 65% more likely to buy from you again," she points out. Regular, meaningful follow-up with past buyers can significantly boost revenue. Keeping customers happy, informed, and feeling appreciated ensures they stick with you, and spend more in the future.

Example

How One Entrepreneur Grew Steadily by Starting Small and Serving Smart

A first-time entrepreneur had a great idea, one they truly believed in. But instead of quitting their job and jumping in headfirst, they took a more strategic route. They knew that success wouldn't come from passion alone; it would require planning, testing, and consistent value creation.

Their journey began with **Tip #1: Start Smart, with Research and a Side Hustle**. Before launching, they spent time researching their target audience, studying the market, and clarifying exactly who they would serve. Rather than diving in full-time, they started small, testing their idea as a side hustle. This gave them the freedom to experiment, adjust, and build confidence while keeping financial stability. As their side venture gained traction, it became clear they were on the right track.

With a foundation in place, they leaned into **Tip #2: Create Relevant, High-Value Content**. Instead of spending heavily on ads, they created a simple yet powerful strategy: educating, engaging, and serving. A weekly blog, helpful social posts, and short videos positioned them as trusted experts. They weren't just promoting a product; they were building a relationship with their audience. As their content reached the right people, inbound interest grew steadily.

But what truly accelerated their growth was **Tip #3: Nurture Your Existing Customers**. Rather than constantly chasing new buyers, they focused on the people who had already said yes. Through thoughtful check-ins, personalized follow-ups, and a commitment to delivering consistent value, they turned one-time buyers into repeat clients and loyal advocates. This community of happy customers became their greatest marketing engine, bringing referrals, testimonials, and ongoing business.

By starting with strategy, serving with intention, and staying connected to the people who mattered most, this entrepreneur didn't just grow a business; they built something sustainable. It wasn't flashy or overnight, but it was real, and it worked.

Questions and Key Takeaways

Key Takeaways from Melinda Emerson:

- Start your business smartly by launching as a side hustle after careful research.
- Develop high-value content that speaks directly to your ideal customer's needs.
- Focus on retaining existing customers, who are more likely to buy again and spend more.

Food for Thought

- What research and preparation should be done before turning a side hustle into a full-time business?
- How do you identify your ideal customer's pain points and create content that truly resonates with them?
- What strategies have been most effective for you in building customer loyalty and encouraging repeat business?

Bio

Guest Expert - Melinda Emerson

Melinda F. Emerson, "SmallBizLady" is America's #1 Small Business Expert. She is a bestselling author, keynote speaker, marketing expert, and business coach. As CEO of Quintessence Group, her marketing consulting firm serves Fortune 500 brands that target the small business market. Her advice is widely read, reaching more than 3 million entrepreneurs each week online. She has an online school, www.smallbizladyuniversity.com, and hosts The Smallbizchat Podcast. She is the bestselling author of Become Your Own Boss in 12 Months, Revised and Expanded.

Section #2

Maximizing Profit

"The Greatest Fear of Many Business Owners," is the key theme in chapter 3 of my first book *Running Your Small Business Like A Pro*. Based on working 1-on-1 with more than one thousand business owners, they fear, avoid, and don't appreciate the importance of both numbers and analysis. As a result, their businesses are not optimized, and they are much less profitable than they should be.

Often, their financial records are inaccurate or untimely, which is a critical first step in maximizing profitability. Even when business owners do have accurate, timely financial information, they do not know how to read their financial statements to access valuable information within them. As a result, they cannot understand how their business really works, and they lack valuable knowledge that would help them make better decisions. Additionally, they lack valuable tools for managing and optimizing their businesses since you cannot improve anything that you do not measure.

I help them overcome their fear of numbers and analysis by helping them understand that they only need to be able to…
- Add
- Subtract
- Multiply
- Divide
- With a calculator

From there, they just need to learn basic accounting, the language of business, so they know which numbers are important, what to do with them, and how to interpret the results.

Fortunately, the experts in this book have proven methods and significant experience with leadership and management best practices to help optimize your business and maximize profitability. That's what makes this section so valuable and relevant for you.

Chapter 16: Business is a Team Sport

Guest Expert: Mel Solomon

"No one does it alone. Business is built on team, strategy, and change." — Mel Solomon

Business, like sports, is never a solo game. Mel Solomon draws on decades of manufacturing leadership to show that every win starts with teamwork, a smart game plan, and relentless adaptation. If you want to scale and sustain your business, you must master these fundamentals.

Tip #1

Build Your Team from the Start

Mel knows true success begins and ends with the team. "There's no one that I know in my lifetime in business that was able to do it alone." Early on, Mel relied on external advisors, fractional experts, and consultants, then gradually transitioned to an internal core group as the business found its footing. The ideal team evolves as the company grows, and leaders must remain flexible and focused on recruiting the right players at each stage.

Tip #2

Always Have (and Adjust) Your Strategy

Great products alone won't make you a winner if you don't have a plan to reach your markets fast. Mel's experience taught him to continually refine distribution and growth strategies by asking: "Where are the markets, and how do I penetrate them quickly?" An efficient and intentional strategy helped Mel's business scale up and introduce new products to new markets ahead of the competition.

Tip # 3

Make Change the Heart of Your Culture

The most successful teams never stop evolving. Mel says, "Change is the key," and he challenges business owners to put change at the very center of their decision-making. Forget, "If it ain't broke, don't fix it", that doesn't work in the real world. Make yourself and your whole organization agents of change, take risks, try new things, and adapt constantly. In Mel's words: "We step to the plate. We swing. Even hitting two out of five is Hall-of-Fame stuff!" Embracing risk and driving changes will keep your business alive and thriving, season after season.

Example

Tip #1: Build Your Team from the Start

When Mel launched his business, he couldn't afford a full staff, so he brought in various external experts, consultants, contractors, and advisors. As cash flow stabilized and operations expanded, he began building an internal team. This evolution taught him to assess and reassess: Who do we need on the team to win today? Who will we need tomorrow? The right mix at each phase helped the company avoid burnout and seize new opportunities quickly.

Tip #2: Always Have (and Adjust) Your Strategy

One year, Mel noticed that competitors were moving into a new market segment. Instead of waiting, he called his team together, analyzed their strengths, and crafted a focused entry plan. By acting quickly and adjusting the strategy as they got feedback, Mel's business captured a significant slice of the segment, demonstrating that strategy is not just about planning, but about executing and adapting at high speed.

Tip #3: Make Change the Heart of Your Culture

To keep the company agile, Mel walked the plant floor looking for process bottlenecks or outdated practices. The team joked that when Mel was seen inspecting with his hands behind his back, it meant something was about to change. Sometimes, his ideas didn't work out, but embracing change, discussing lessons, and taking another swing built a culture where innovation was a team sport, not a risky solo act.

Key Takeaways and Food for Thought

Key Takeaways from Mel Solomon:

- Team is everything. Success requires people who share the vision and evolve with the company.
- Strategy drives growth. Identify markets, enter them fast, and scale with profitability.
- Change is constant. Make a change in your core mindset, accept risks, and lead evolution.

Food for Thought

- How often do you step back and ask: Is this the right team for where we're going next?
- Is your business strategy nimble enough to enter new markets quickly, or are you too slow to pivot?
- What would it look like if your company truly celebrated change, even when it meant making mistakes along the way?

Bio

Guest Expert - Mel Solomon

Mel Solomon is the former owner of Tri-Arc Manufacturing, based in Pittsburgh, Pennsylvania. He acquired Tri-Arc in 1992 along with Fred Schwartz and has since led the company to provide a diverse range of fall protection and access products to multiple industries, including oil and gas, manufacturing, aviation, and aerospace.

Under his leadership, Tri-Arc has become recognized for safety, durability, and code-compliance solutions, successfully establishing itself as a trusted provider in the market. After successfully scaling and ultimately selling Tri-Arc, Mel is now retired.

Chapter 17: Scaling Your Business in 2025

Guest Expert: Clevonne St. Hillaire

"Bet on yourself — and be willing to take risks."
— *Clevonne St. Hillaire*

Scaling a business isn't just about getting bigger, it's about getting better, smarter, and more focused. In our conversation, entrepreneur and business strategist Clevonne St. Hillaire shared powerful advice for business owners who are ready to take their next big leap in 2025 and beyond.

His three lessons cut straight to the heart of what it takes to grow: belief, discipline, and community.

Tip #1

Bet on Yourself and Take Strategic Risks

The first and most crucial mindset shift, according to Clevonne, is to **believe in yourself** fully.

Scaling a business requires risk. It demands that you step outside your comfort zone and sometimes go against the grain. You may not always follow the conventional path, and that's okay. What matters most is that you recognize the ability you already have within you to achieve your goals.

"You have the ability within you to do whatever is in your heart to do," Clevonne emphasized. Taking risks isn't optional; it's essential.

Without bold moves, there's no real progress. Trust yourself enough to invest your time, energy, and resources into your vision, even when it feels uncomfortable.

Tip #2

Track Everything: Inputs, Outputs, and Results

The second key to scaling successfully is developing the discipline to **track everything** in your business.

Clevonne encouraged entrepreneurs to measure both their efforts and their results, not just the big wins, but also the small actions.

Every marketing campaign, networking event, client conversation, and investment costs something, time, money, and energy, and you need to know if the return is worth it.

"If it makes sense to keep doing it, keep doing it," Clevonne said. "If it doesn't, cut it out."

This clear-eyed evaluation is critical. Scaling isn't just about doing more; it's about doing more of what works and less of what doesn't.

In short: **Track it. Measure it. Adjust accordingly.**

Tip # 3

Surround Yourself with Mentors and Growth-Minded People

Finally, Clevonne stressed the importance of **community and mentorship**.

No one scales a business alone.

Surrounding yourself with people who are already doing what you aspire to do is one of the most powerful accelerators for growth.

Clevonne credited much of his progress to mentors and industry peers who offered encouragement, advice, and tough love when needed. They helped him refine his leadership skills, improve his business strategies, and see possibilities he might have missed on his own.

"You need people who see the potential in you, and who challenge you to keep growing," he shared.

Find mentors. Connect with peers who are a step or two ahead of you. Stay close to people who inspire action, not just talk.

Example

How One Entrepreneur Scaled by Taking Risks, Tracking Results, and Building a Growth Circle

A driven entrepreneur had reached a turning point. Growth felt stalled, and despite working hard, the business wasn't scaling the way they'd hoped. Instead of retreating, they decided to embrace a new mindset, one centered around belief, discipline, and community.

It began with **Tip #1: Bet on Yourself and Take Strategic Risks**. Instead of waiting for perfect conditions or external validation, they chose to trust their instincts. They stepped outside their comfort zone, investing in new marketing, launching offers before they felt "ready," and pitching themselves for bigger opportunities. It wasn't about recklessness; it was about bold, intentional action. The moment they bet on themselves, momentum shifted. Confidence grew, and with it came new doors opening.

Next came **Tip #2: Track Everything, Inputs, Outputs, and Results**. They started paying close attention to what was moving the needle. Every client lead, every social post, every dollar spent was tracked. They didn't just measure success in revenue; they evaluated the effort it took to get there. Some strategies stayed, others were cut. By reviewing what worked and what didn't, the business began to grow more efficiently, not just faster. Less time was wasted, and more energy was directed toward what delivered real results.

The real game-changer, though, was **Tip #3: Surround Yourself with Mentors and Growth-Minded People**. Realizing that solo effort only took them so far, they intentionally sought out a circle of ambitious peers and experienced mentors. These connections became a sounding board, a source of tough feedback, and a well of inspiration. Through regular conversations, masterminds, and coaching, they stayed accountable and encouraged. Being around people who expected more, and believed more, helped this entrepreneur keep raising the bar.

By betting on themselves, staying data-driven, and aligning with a strong community, they didn't just grow a business; they built something that could truly scale.

Questions and Key Takeaways

Key Takeaways from Clevonne St. Hillaire:

- Believe in yourself fully and be willing to take strategic risks.
- Track every input and output to make smarter business decisions.
- Surround yourself with mentors and peers who push you to grow.

Food for Thought

- What mindset shifts or support systems could help you build greater self-belief and the courage to take smart, calculated risks?
- How can you set up simple, effective systems to consistently track your efforts and results, and what patterns might this data reveal to guide better decisions?
- What qualities should you look for in mentors and peers, and how can you actively cultivate a network that challenges and supports your growth?

Bio

Guest Expert - Clevonne St. Hillaire

Clevonne St. Hillaire is a results-oriented and well-organized Engineer with over 16 years of experience. As an innovative leader, he has a proven track record of developing and executing both technical and strategic plans, with a strong emphasis on security, building strong relationships, and resolving conflicts effectively. Clevonne's expertise spans technological development, change management, and digital transformation. He is a convincing communicator and keen observer, known for his exceptional organizational, administrative, and management skills.

After working with Verizon for 10 years, Clevonne transitioned last year to work full-time in his family business, aiming to grow significantly in 2025. We've been collaborating closely, discussing strategies, and exploring opportunities for substantial growth this year.

Chapter 18: Double Your Close Rate Will Multiply Your Profit

Guest Expert: Doug C. Brown

"Client acquisition is your business, not just a task. Master it and selling will never be your bottleneck." — Doug C. Brown

Doug C. Brown, CEO of CEO Sales Strategies and a sales profit acceleration expert, has helped entrepreneurs and Fortune 500 companies alike make sales their superpower.

In this chapter, Doug reveals that consistent business growth comes down to three simple but powerful practices: never stop acquiring clients, always clarify your ideal buyer, and prioritize selling above all else.

Tip #1

Know What Business You're In, Client Acquisition

Doug stresses that regardless of your size or industry, you're really in the client acquisition business. Mastering lead generation and conversion isn't just "a" job for entrepreneurs; it is the job. As you refine this foundational skill, your confidence grows, your sales pipeline stays full, and you leapfrog competitors who focus mainly on operations or fulfillment.

Tip #2

Know Your Ideal Client (Right Fit Buyer)

Trying to sell to everyone wastes time, energy, and money. Doug recommends regularly profiling your happiest, highest-spending, and most easily converted clients. Interview them to understand exactly why they purchased, then use those answers to replicate your best results. If you're just starting out, AI tools can help you brainstorm ideal customer traits and FAQs.

Tip # 3

Sell, Sell, Sell, Relentlessly

For most businesses, especially in early stages, 90% of your attention should be on selling. Even as you grow, keep at least 80% of your focus on marketing, selling, and closing. Lead flow plus workflow equals cash flow: keep your pipeline strong, close every qualified lead you can, and sales momentum will fuel every other part of your business.

Example

Tip #1: Know What Business You're In, Client Acquisition

A small B2B consulting firm that previously focused almost solely on delivering projects shifted its mindset to prioritize weekly outbound lead generation and sales follow-up. Within three months, not only did their client roster grow, but they found themselves saying "no" to lower-fit clients and filling the pipeline with better prospects.

Tip #2: Know Your Ideal Client (Right Fit Buyer)

The consulting firm analyzed existing clients and found their most profitable, easiest-to-please customers all shared similar industries, company sizes, and pain points. By interviewing these clients, they discovered key motivators, speed, communication, and specific business ROI. They then adapted their marketing and sales language to align with those motivations, further improving their close rates.

Tip #3: Sell, Sell, Sell, Relentlessly

Instead of splitting efforts between admin, product work, and cold outreach, the founder allocated 80% of their week to sales calls, networking, and proposal follow-ups. The focus paid off, monthly revenue quickly doubled, and profit margins soared because they were selling intentionally to the right audience.

Questions and Key Takeaways

Key Takeaways from Doug C. Brown:

- Focus relentlessly on client acquisition as your core business.
- Identify and interview your best-fit clients, let them shape your sales priorities.
- Keep most of your time and team energy on selling to sustain revenue and profit growth.

Food for Thought

- How much time are you dedicating each week to active client acquisition, and how could you double it?
- Who are your current "dream clients," and what insights can you uncover to replicate your best results?
- Does your daily calendar reflect that sales is your #1 priority, or are you getting distracted by lower-value tasks?

Bio

Guest Expert - Doug C. Brown

Doug C. Brown is an international bestselling author, sales growth expert, and CEO of CEO Sales Strategies, renowned for helping organizations double their close rates and multiply profits.

He has led high-impact sales programs for industry giants, including Intuit, CBS Television, and Procter & Gamble, and previously directed Tony Robbins and Chet Holmes' sales training division with record success.

With over $500 million in sales generated and more than 35 companies built, Doug is recognized for his results-driven strategies and leadership in sales revenue optimization.

Chapter 19: Outsourcing to Save Time & Make More Money

Guest Expert: Gene Bohensky

"In order for you to grow your business and grow as a person, you need to hire an assistant sooner rather than later."
— Gene Bohensky

Gene Bohensky, a seasoned entrepreneur and operations expert, shares the secret to scaling without burning out: outsourcing. If you're doing everything yourself, you're limiting your business growth. Gene explains why learning to delegate is not optional; it's a necessary shift to free up your time, amplify your results, and position your business for bigger success.

Tip #1

Hire an Assistant Sooner Than You Think

Gene's first key lesson is clear: don't wait too long to get help. "You need to hire an assistant sooner rather than later," he says. Learning how to delegate tasks early is essential if you want to grow personally and professionally. Hiring help isn't a luxury; it's a fundamental step toward scaling your business effectively.

Tip #2

Inventory Your Tasks and Outsource Smartly

You may not even realize how much of your day is filled with tasks someone else could handle. Gene stresses the importance of listing everything you do; plus the things you wish you had time to do. Once you see the full picture, you'll understand how much time you're wasting and how much faster you could grow by delegating properly.

Tip # 3

Find the Right Assistant Through the Right Source

Not all outsourcing options are created equal. Gene advises business owners to be strategic about where they hire their assistants from. Whether it's agencies or direct hires, look for firms that guarantee committed, high-quality workers. A stable, reliable assistant will save you countless headaches and help create a lasting support system for your business.

Example

How One Business Owner Unlocked Growth by Delegating, Outsourcing, and Hiring the Right Help

At first, they thought they could do it all, emails, client calls, marketing, and administrative work. But as the business picked up speed, so did the burnout. Every hour was filled, and growth started to stall. That's when they decided to make a pivotal change.

It began with **Tip #1: Hire an Assistant Sooner Than You Think**. Instead of waiting until they were overwhelmed, they brought someone on board while things were still manageable. It wasn't easy to let go of control, but once they did, the shift was immediate. With support in place, they finally had the breathing room to focus on strategy, growth, and revenue-generating activities.

Then came **Tip #2: Inventory Your Tasks and Outsource Smartly**. They took a hard look at their to-do list, not just the tasks they were doing, but also the ones they were neglecting. From scheduling to social media to customer follow-ups, they identified what could be delegated and matched each task to someone better suited for the job. Time was no longer slipping through the cracks; it was being invested more wisely.

The breakthrough happened with **Tip #3: Find the Right Assistant Through the Right Source**. Rather than hiring randomly, they vetted options carefully, partnering with a service that specialized in experienced, dedicated support. The result? A dependable assistant who didn't just "help", they became an extension of the business. Reliable, skilled, and aligned with the company's goals, this assistant made daily operations smoother and growth more sustainable.

By learning to delegate early, outsourcing with intention, and investing in the right support, this business owner didn't just gain time; they gained momentum. The business didn't just get easier to run; it became poised to scale.

Questions and Key Takeaways

Key Takeaways from Gene Bohensky:

- Hire an assistant early to learn the art of delegation.
- List your daily and aspirational tasks to find what should be outsourced.
- Choose high-quality assistants through trustworthy sources for lasting success.

Food for Thought

- How could bringing on an assistant early help you practice effective delegation and free up your time for higher-impact activities?
- What tasks in your current and future workload could be delegated to others, and how would outsourcing them help you focus on your core strengths?
- What criteria and sourcing strategies can you use to select assistants who align with your needs, values, and long-term goals?

Bio

Guest Expert - Gene Bohensky

Gene Bohensky, CEO of Archer Contact Solution, an outsourced service in the Philippines that was launched in 2023. The company has successfully hired more than 100 people, and the plan is to have 1,000 employees. Additionally, more than 10 years ago, he founded Archer Strategies to assist companies in developing and refining their sales processes to achieve outstanding results. He works with select B-to-B clients to help target the right audience for their specific product or service and then helps them craft the right message to start meaningful sales conversations. In short, he gets you solid sales leads, with a particular emphasis on developing winning programs for technical and innovative products.

Chapter 20: How To Boost Profit with Operational Excellence

Guest Expert: Josh Tan

"Set time to measure, plan to solve problems, and make your team the engine of accountability." — Josh Tan

Josh Tan, a heart-centered executive coach and strategic consultant, believes profit comes from operational discipline, not just clever ideas. His approach to operational excellence enables boosting profit as a repeatable habit, built on measuring what matters, proactively identifying and eliminating problems, and fostering genuine team accountability.

Tip #1

Set Time to Measure

Nearly every business owner knows they should "measure their numbers." Josh points out that most miss the mark simply because they don't set aside dedicated time for it. Commit regular blocks, weekly, monthly, or even daily, to review your operational objectives. Only by putting metrics on the calendar do they become a guiding force in decision-making, allowing for proactive moves that directly impact your bottom line.

Tip #2

Plan to Solve and Predict Problems

Great operational leaders don't just track new initiatives; they plan for which problems must be stopped. Josh's advice: Take time to identify stubborn issues, bottlenecks, or potential pitfalls and carve out space to solve them each week. Even better, make a habit of predicting which problems could be coming next, then act to prevent them before they arise. Operational excellence is as much about "what to discontinue" as "what to start."

Tip # 3

Make Accountability a Team Sport

Solo efforts can't support consistent excellence. Josh recommends daily or weekly team huddles, not just to share updates, but to create a space where team members are invited to spot issues, suggest improvements, and hold each other (including you, the owner) accountable. The more voices you encourage, the less likely errors or warning signs are to slip through the cracks. A culture of collaborative accountability turns "problems" into group solutions and fuels growth.

Example

Tip #1: Set Time to Measure

A boutique retailer struggling with slim margins scheduled a fixed time every Monday morning just to review inventory turnover and weekly sales metrics. After a month, trend patterns emerged, allowing them to double down on bestsellers while proactively clearing slow movers, directly boosting cash flow and profit.

Tip #2: Plan to Solve and Predict Problems

The store owner noticed recurring order delays and returns. Instead of waiting for the next crisis, she listed these as "problems to solve," dedicating time to tackle the root cause and then brainstorming future issues as a team. Foreseeing potential holiday supply shortages, she preordered seasonal products, preventing lost sales and customer frustration.

Tip #3: Make Accountability a Team Sport

The retailer adopted a 10-minute daily huddle where the staff could highlight yesterday's wins, flag new bottlenecks, and suggest quick fixes. One assistant flagged an inventory mismatch that would have cost thousands, and by tackling it together, the team saved time and improved morale, transforming little problems into teachable moments.

Questions and Key Takeaways

Key Takeaways from Josh Tan:

- Regular, scheduled measurement turns "should do" into daily profit habits.
- Planning to solve (and anticipate) operational problems ensures smoother growth.
- Team-driven accountability uncovers and fixes issues faster than solo management ever could.

Food for Thought

- When is your next recurring "measurement session" and whose calendar is it on?
- What stubborn problems are you tolerating right now, and what's your plan to predict and prevent new ones?
- How can you make your team more proactive in spotting and solving operational hiccups before they impact profit?

Bio

Guest Expert - Josh Tan

Josh Tan is a passionate entrepreneur focused on growing and scaling small companies. His background includes ten years of experience in manufacturing engineering and operational management, with a focus on enhancing efficiency, increasing profitability, and reducing failures.

After his engineering career, he launched a private consulting practice serving small businesses across various industries. Josh is now the COO of a medical device company that focuses on delivering high-value products and systems to our healthcare provider clients. They concentrate on Wound Care products and devices.

Chapter 21: Strategies for Well-being and Effective Leadership

Guest Expert: Vanessa Zamy

"Burnout culture is not your only option, defibrillate your life to revive your energy for real growth." — Vanessa Zamy

Vanessa Zamy, known as The Business Defibrillator®, is a catalyst for transformative change within organizations. As Managing Principal of LiberationX Contracts, Vanessa leads her nationwide team of trainers to empower leaders and executives by building high-performing teams and navigating the complexities of the modern workplace.

Tip #1

Lead Beyond the Numbers

Vanessa insists that business is about more than finance; it's about leadership. If you've been in business for five years or more, it's time to consider hiring your first employee or, if you already have a team, deepening your leadership through regular, personal one-on-one check-ins.

These aren't just about project updates. Instead, ask: Where are your team members with their goals? How do they feel about their contribution? What do they want to grow into? Leadership is also about unlocking your people's vision, not just their output.

Tip #2

Communicate Through Active Listening

Effective leadership, Vanessa explains, is rooted in communication, especially active listening. She encourages leaders to step into real conversations with employees, especially those considered "difficult." Are they entrepreneurial thinkers or doers? Ask thoughtful questions, listen carefully, and avoid micromanagement.

By understanding your employees' thoughts and needs, you turn even challenging relationships into valuable partnerships and keep your workforce engaged and motivated.

Tip # 3

Prioritize Your Own Well-being

Finally, burnout is the enemy of both life and business. Vanessa boldly rejects "hustle culture." Instead, she teaches entrepreneurs to proactively protect their well-being. "Stress kills, and hustle isn't sustainable," she warns. The key: regularly reflect on what brings you joy, laughter, and peace, then intentionally build more of it into your routine. When you show up whole, your business thrives.

Example

Tip #1: Lead Beyond the Numbers

After five years running a solo consulting business, Sarah decided to hire her first assistant. Instead of only tracking finances, she began scheduling monthly one-on-one coffee chats, asking about her new teammate's dreams and where she wanted to grow in the company. These open conversations sparked a sense of ownership and led to improved collaboration and innovative ideas from her team.

Tip #2: Communicate Through Active Listening

When Sarah noticed friction with a "difficult" employee, she took Vanessa's advice and asked herself: Was this person a doer, or an entrepreneur at heart? By inviting honest dialogue and carefully listening, rather than just giving directions, Sarah discovered that her employee had a host of untapped ideas. Shifting from micromanaging to collaborating changed their working relationship and team dynamics.

Tip #3: Prioritize Your Own Well-being

Sarah realized she was running on empty and losing enthusiasm for her business. Instead of pushing harder, she reflected on what brought her genuine joy: weekly walks with her dog and Saturday dinners with friends. By reintroducing those into her schedule, she started showing up to work more energized, optimistic, and able to support her team with renewed creativity.

Questions and Key Takeaways

Key Takeaways from Vanessa Zamy:

- Go beyond the numbers, lead by understanding your team's goals and dreams.
- Use active listening and curiosity to transform workplace relationships.
- Make self-care and true joy a non-negotiable part of your entrepreneurial routine.

Food for Thought

- When was the last time you had a development-focused, not just task-focused, conversation with a team member?
- How could better listening, not just talking, improve your most challenging employee relationships?
- What's one joyful activity you can schedule this week to recharge your energy for both life and business?

Bio

Guest Expert - Vanessa Zamy

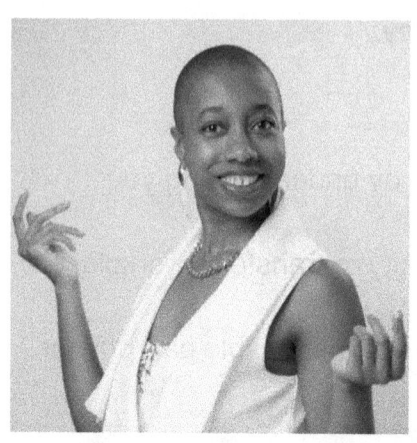

Vanessa Zamy, known as The Business Defibrillator®, is a catalyst for transformative change within organizations. As Managing Principal of LiberationX Contracts, Vanessa leads a nationwide team of trainers and coaches who help leaders build high-performing teams able to navigate the modern workplace.

Vanessa brings a wealth of experience working with diverse organizations, from Fortune 500 companies and public sector agencies to small businesses and startups. She excels as a global dynamic speaker, leadership trainer, and HR strategist, driving meaningful shifts in mindset and performance across all levels and industries.

Vanessa Zamy's powerful insights have been featured in esteemed publications, including Fast Company and NPR Marketplace, affirming her status as a thought leader in corporate wellness and leadership development. Vanessa's personal journey from adversity to triumph serves as a compelling testament to her unwavering determination, unparalleled expertise, and unmatched performance prowess.

Chapter 22: Financial Management Triage for Entrepreneurs

Guest Expert: Jeneen Perkins

"If you see negative numbers, don't wait. Get help."
— *Jeneen Perkins*

When it comes to running a business, financial management isn't optional; it's survival. Jeneen Perkins, a seasoned accountant and financial strategist, knows this reality firsthand. In our conversation, she shared three crucial lessons that every entrepreneur must master to build a resilient and successful business.

Tip #1

Substantiate to Alleviate Your Tax Burden

One of the first things Jeneen stressed was the importance of **substantiating** your financial activity. As a business owner, it's not enough to feel like you're making good decisions; you must prove it, especially when it comes to taxes.

Every dollar that enters or exits your business should be clearly documented. Jeneen advises entrepreneurs to **organize and digitize** their records whenever possible. If handling paper feels overwhelming, consider taking a photo of receipts and uploading them to a secure cloud drive. The goal is simple: make your records easy to find, easy to understand, and impossible to lose.

Solid documentation not only alleviates your tax burden but also gives you clarity and control over your business operations. The more organized you are, the less stressful tax season and business ownership will be.

Tip #2

Don't Ignore Red Flags in Your Financials

Another critical point Jeneen made was about **recognizing when you need help**. If you notice negative numbers anywhere on your financial statements, it's a red flag you can't afford to ignore.

"Get help". Negative figures usually point to deeper issues that are likely outside your expertise. Waiting too long can make a fix far more costly or even impossible.

Hiring a professional accountant or financial consultant at the first sign of trouble can be the difference between a business that recovers and one that fails. Sometimes, the smartest move isn't to try to figure everything out on your own. It's knowing when to call in a specialist.

Tip # 3

Plan and Budget Like Your Success Depends on It (Because It Does)

Finally, Jeneen emphasized the importance of **strategizing and planning** for success. No matter how skilled you are at the technical side of your business, a thoughtful business plan and a well-structured budget are non-negotiable essentials.

Jeneen admitted that even for her, an accountant by trade, planning and budgeting aren't always the most exciting parts of entrepreneurship. But she forces herself to do it because she knows that consistent planning is the foundation of growth and sustainability.

"Even if you don't want to do it, you have to do it," she shared. Setting financial expectations for your business and holding yourself accountable to them creates a clear roadmap to success. Without it, you're operating blindly, and the risks multiply.

Example

How One Business Owner Transformed Their Finances by Documenting Diligently, Catching Red Flags, and Planning with Purpose

At first, their business looked fine on the surface — sales were coming in, clients seemed happy, and things felt… busy. But deep down, they had a nagging sense that their financial foundation wasn't as strong as it should be. The books were messy, tax season was stressful, and they couldn't answer simple questions about profit or cash flow without digging through piles of receipts.

Everything began to shift with **Tip #1: Substantiate to Alleviate Your Tax Burden**. They realized that being "organized enough" wasn't cutting it. So they committed to documenting everything — every invoice, expense, and transaction. They stopped throwing receipts in drawers and started scanning and uploading them into a cloud folder. What felt like a small change gave them massive peace of mind. When tax season came, they were ready — no scrambling, no guesswork. With clean records, they felt more in control and finally understood where their money was really going.

Then came **Tip #2: Don't Ignore Red Flags in Your Financials**. One month, a quick glance at their statements revealed a negative cash flow trend. Before, they might have brushed it off or tried to "fix it later." But this time, they acted fast — reaching out to a financial consultant to dive into the numbers. That one conversation uncovered inefficient spending, underpriced services, and overdue invoices. Fixing those issues helped them plug financial leaks before they became sinkholes. What could've been a disaster turned into a wake-up call that protected their business.

The final step was embracing **Tip #3: Plan and Budget Like Your Success Depends on It (Because It Does)**. Budgeting wasn't something they enjoyed — but they finally understood how essential it was. They carved out time each month to map out expected income, plan major expenses, and set clear financial targets. The discipline of planning gave them direction. Instead of reacting to emergencies, they were making proactive, strategic moves — and watching their profits grow.

By getting organized, acting on warning signs, and staying financially intentional, this entrepreneur didn't just clean up their books — they built a stronger, smarter, more resilient business.

Questions and Key Takeaways

Key Takeaways from Jeneen Perkins:

- Organize and digitize your financial records to stay ready for tax season.
- Seek professional help immediately when you spot negative numbers.
- Prioritize strategic planning and budgeting, even when it feels difficult.

Food for Thought

- What systems or tools can you set up now to keep your financial records organized and easily accessible throughout the year?
- How can you recognize early warning signs in your finances, and what steps should you take to bring in expert support before problems escalate?
- What habits or mindsets could help you stay committed to regular strategic planning and budgeting, especially during busy or stressful periods?

Bio

Guest Expert - Jeneen Perkins

Jeneen Perkins is a fractional controller and the CEO of Eclat Enterprises, a full-service accounting firm located in Wisconsin. In August of 2011, Jeneen launched Eclat Enterprises to serve entrepreneurs, small businesses, and non-profits by providing accounting and tax services in "plain" English.

In previous years, Jeneen served as a certified mentor for SCORE as a volunteer for the Southeast Wisconsin chapter and mentored over 20 entrepreneurs and startups. Currently, Eclat Enterprises offers many services, including startup and compliance consulting, small business accounting, and real estate accounting services

Chapter 23: 3 Things That Can Improve Your Risk Profile

Guest Expert: Paul Paray

"Protect what's valuable — your business depends on it."
— *Paul Paray*

As a small business owner and attorney with experience helping victims of data breaches and intellectual property theft, Paul Paray has seen firsthand how even savvy business owners make costly mistakes when it comes to protecting their intellectual capital. In our conversation, he shared three areas where a lack of attention leads to serious exposures, and how entrepreneurs can protect themselves before problems arise.

His advice blends legal protection, data security, and the power of community learning.

Tip #1

Don't Assume Your Employees Have Good Email Hygiene

In today's digital world, cybersecurity isn't just an IT issue; it's a matter of survival.

Paul's first warning was simple but urgent: **Never assume your employees know how to spot email threats**. Mass phishing exploits and targeted spear phishing attacks are now automated, increasingly sophisticated, and frequently rely on AI to fool employees into giving up their credentials. A single careless click can compromise your entire business network, resulting in devastating financial and reputational losses.

Train your team on basic email hygiene by having them understand how to recognize suspicious emails and why it's important to avoid clicking on unknown links or downloading images and files. Understanding and reporting these exploits is no longer optional. It's essential.

Cybersecurity awareness must become part of your corporate culture, starting from the top down.

Tip #2

Protect Your Intellectual Property

The second pitfall Paul highlighted in his talk is the failure to recognize and **protect intellectual property (IP)**.

Too many business owners focus solely on selling their products or services without concern about the underlying assets that really make their brand valuable.

When Paul noticed a "TM" (trademark) next to one of our services during our discussion, he immediately emphasized how critical it is to formalize protection by filing a federal trademark application rather than just relying on common law protections.

Your trademarks, copyrights, inventions, and even business processes can become financial assets if properly protected and are part of your business. These assets not only help you compete but can significantly increase the value of your business when you seek investment, partnerships, and exit opportunities.

According to the SBA, more than half of the nation's small-business owners are over the age of 50, and approximately 21% of the US population was born before 1964. Founders sometimes ignore the fact that one day they will be too old to continue managing a successful business. One metric used in valuing businesses is tied to a company's ability to scale based on its protected intellectual property assets. In other words, sustainable growth is not always about making more; it's also about being able to protect what you've already built.

In short, if you've created something unique, **protect it** so that you can later sell it as part of your business.

Tip # 3

Join Associations and Leverage Free Resources

Finally, Paul stressed the importance of at least tapping into **community and government resources** when there are budget concerns. Entrepreneurs thrive when they connect with others facing similar challenges. By joining industry associations, networking groups, and professional organizations, you gain access to shared wisdom, new opportunities, and valuable resources at a low cost.

He specifically recommended tapping into free tools from trusted sources like the **National Institute of Standards and Technology (NIST)** and the **Small Business Administration (SBA),** both of which offer extensive materials on cybersecurity best practices tailored for small businesses. In fact, NIST helps companies with no cybersecurity plans in place "kick-start their cybersecurity risk management strategy" with the NIST Cybersecurity Framework 2.0.

Learning from others and using available resources isn't a luxury, it's a strategic move that is smart and cost-effective.

Example

From Vulnerable to Vigilant: How Four Partners Fortified Their Company for Long-Term Success

After 14 years of steady growth, partners in a thriving small business began having concerns about data security, unprotected IP assets, and an overwhelming sense that the business wasn't fully protected. This realization began after a bank partner asked probing questions that they could not answer. What began as low-grade anxiety hit a peak when a team member unknowingly clicked on a suspicious email. It was ultimately a close call, and a wake-up call.

The business owners embraced **Tip #1: Don't Assume Your Employees Have Good Email Hygiene**. They realized that while their team was talented and hardworking, no one had ever been trained on how to spot phishing emails or avoid dangerous links. Rather than blaming the employee, they invested in a company-wide cybersecurity training program provided by an online outside vendor. What started as a defensive move turned into a cultural shift. Security awareness became a shared value, not just a checklist item. It even became fun for employees, given the competitive spirit of the training.

With that foundation in place, it was time to address **Tip #2: Protect Your Intellectual Property**. As they reviewed the content and systems powering their business, everything from brand names to training materials, they saw just how much value was going unguarded. They consulted a legal expert, began securing trademarks and copyrights, and created protection for confidential materials. The process wasn't quick or glamorous, but it gave them something priceless: ownership, leverage, and peace of mind.

Finally, they tapped into **Tip #3: Join Associations and Leverage Free Resources**. The founders connected even deeper with member local and national trade organizations by seeking available expert guidance. They also reviewed cybersecurity tools from NIST, which confirmed they were doing things the right way and helped them better understand vulnerabilities, implement stronger protections, and stay updated on emerging threats. What once felt overwhelming started to become manageable, even empowering, especially after they realized they didn't have to figure it all out alone.

Six months later, the business was in a different place entirely: safer, stronger, and more scalable. The founders could focus on growth, knowing that the business was better protected from data and IP risks and was ready for a potential sale, which occurred a few years later!

Their journey proved a critical point: real growth isn't just about making more; it's about protecting what you've already built. With the right systems, support, and mindset, entrepreneurs can go from vulnerable to vigilant, and in the process create a business that's built to grow and last.

Questions and Key Takeaways

Key Takeaways from Paul Paray:

- Train your employees on good email hygiene to avoid cybersecurity threats.
- Protect your intellectual property early to safeguard your business's future value.
- Join associations and use free resources to stay informed and protected.

Food for Thought

- What are the ways your business educates employees about email safety to reduce the risk of cyberattacks?
- What steps do you take to ensure your intellectual property is fully protected as your business grows?
- In what ways have you used industry associations and free resources to better understand data security and regulatory challenges?

Bio

Guest Expert - Paul Paray

Paul is a founder of Licenz, LLC, an online provider of compliance services, and has a diverse legal and business background that includes creating resilient security and privacy compliance programs; successfully building intellectual property portfolios; successfully litigating federal and state commercial and IP disputes around the country; and helping small and mid-sized business owners navigate numerous risk management issues. To that end, he has been invited to speak at leading conferences to discuss risk management, including RSA, IAPP, RIMS and PLUS, and has been interviewed regarding compliance and risk management by the National Law Journal, Business Insurance, CFO Magazine, ComputerWorld, SC Magazine, Security Management, The Financial Post, The Hartford Business Journal, The Newark Star-Ledger, New Jersey Law Journal, and The New York Times.

Chapter 24: The Top Financial Mistakes Entrepreneurs Make

Special Guest: Perry Nunes

"You don't know what you don't track." — Perry Nunes

Perry Nunes, a representative at the small business banking platform called Found.com, highlights a hard truth: many entrepreneurs fail financially not because they aren't working hard, but because they aren't managing their money strategically. In this chapter, Perry shares actionable ways to get control of your finances without getting overwhelmed. His advice demonstrates how financial clarity can become your most significant growth lever.

Tip #1

Track Your Money Consistently

"You don't know what you don't track," Perry emphasizes. Entrepreneurs must overcome the tendency to avoid financial details by regularly reviewing their income and expenses. Tracking your financials, ideally on a weekly basis, helps you build an accurate profit and loss statement (P&L) and spot trends early. The key is to make it a habit, not a once-a-year panic session.

Tip #2

Automate Financial Processes Wherever Possible

Don't rely on memory or manual labor to manage your money. Perry advises finding tools that automatically categorize expenses and set aside savings for taxes. Automation removes human error and makes staying financially healthy almost effortless. Whether it's using apps that automatically sort transactions or setting up a separate tax savings account, smart automation is essential.

Tip # 3

Start Small and Improve as You Go

Instead of waiting for the "perfect system," Perry encourages entrepreneurs just to start. Experiment with free tools and simple processes to get momentum. "Test things out... don't be afraid to change course," he advises. Financial management evolves with your business, so be flexible and willing to upgrade your systems over time.

Example

The Money Turnaround: How One Business Owner Built Financial Confidence from Scratch

In the early stages of running their business, a talented service provider was great at what they did but avoided anything that looked like bookkeeping. Receipts piled up. Invoices were scattered. Tax time was a nightmare. They figured if the bank account wasn't empty, things were "fine." But deep down, they knew that winging it wasn't sustainable.

Everything began to shift with **Tip #1: Track Your Money Consistently**. They committed to reviewing income and expenses every week, even if it felt uncomfortable at first. With every check-in, they got a clearer picture of where the money was going. Some offerings were barely breaking even. Others were surprisingly profitable. That weekly habit built confidence and clarity, not just in their finances, but in their decision-making.

Next came **Tip #2: Automate Financial Processes Wherever Possible**. Tired of losing receipts and forgetting due dates, they set up apps that categorized expenses, scheduled invoices, and automatically saved for taxes. The mental load lightened almost immediately. Automation didn't replace their awareness; it supported it, giving them space to focus on growing the business instead of putting out fires.

Finally, they embraced **Tip #3: Start Small and Improve as You Go**. Instead of getting stuck searching for the "perfect" system, they just began. A free app here, a spreadsheet there, small steps that grew into a solid financial foundation. Over time, they upgraded tools, refined processes, and even brought in a bookkeeper. But it all started with the willingness to begin before feeling fully ready.

Today, this entrepreneur isn't just making money; they know where every dollar goes, how much they can reinvest, and when they're ready to scale. What once felt intimidating is now a strength.

The takeaway? You don't need to master finance overnight. With consistent tracking, simple automation, and a willingness to evolve, financial clarity is possible and powerful.

Questions and Key Takeaways

Key Takeaways from Perry Nunes:

- Track both your expenses and income consistently to maintain financial clarity.
- Utilize automation tools to simplify and streamline financial management.
- Start with small financial systems and improve them over time.

Food for Thought

- What strategies have worked best for you in maintaining consistent tracking of both income and expenses?
- How can automation tools help small business owners better manage their finances without getting overwhelmed?
- What are some simple financial systems a new business can implement right away, and how can they be scaled as the business grows?

Bio

Special Guest - Perry Nunes

Perry Nunes works on the growth team at Found, a banking and bookkeeping app for small business owners. He brings nearly a decade of experience supporting and scaling fintech startups and thinks extensively about how to best support small businesses through improved technology, processes, and education.

Found is a financial technology company, not a bank. Business banking services are provided by Piermont Bank, a member of the Federal Deposit Insurance Corporation (FDIC).

Chapter 25: Protect Your Assets with Copyrights & Patents

Guest Expert: Benjamin Dach, Ph.D., J.D.

"Keep organized, file early, and don't be afraid to reach out for help." — Benjamin Dach, Ph.D., J.D.

In today's competitive landscape, protecting your intellectual property is vital to the longevity and success of your business. Benjamin Dach, an expert in intellectual property law, shares essential strategies for safeguarding your business assets with copyrights and patents. As an entrepreneur, understanding the importance of these protections can help you avoid costly mistakes and maintain control over your creations.

Benjamin's top takeaways focus on documentation, timely filing, and seeking legal counsel to ensure that your business ideas and inventions are properly protected.

Tip #1

Keep Diligent Notes

Benjamin's first tip is **to keep organized records** of everything.

It may seem obvious, but consistently tracking your ideas and the dates when they were conceived is an essential step in protecting your intellectual property. "Keep notes, keep track of what you're doing, and keep them organized," Benjamin stresses. This helps ensure you have solid documentation to prove ownership if any disputes arise down the road. Whether you're working on an invention, writing content, or developing a brand, diligent note-taking is crucial for safeguarding your business assets.

For enhanced credibility, Benjamin also suggests using dated lab notebooks or digital timestamping tools to add an extra layer of verification to your documentation. This systematic record-keeping process ensures you always know where you stand with your intellectual property.

Tip #2

File Early

The second key takeaway is to **file your copyrights and patents as early as possible**.

Delaying your filings can leave you vulnerable to others who may try to claim ownership of your ideas or inventions. Benjamin recommends getting your protection in place as soon as you can while still maintaining the quality of your application. "File early," he says, "and make sure you have the necessary protections in place."

Under the "first-to-file" system in patent law, the first person to file a patent application generally has the legal right to the invention, making early filing even more crucial. By securing your intellectual property rights early on, you help prevent others from copying or infringing on your work. Filing early ensures you have a legal claim to your intellectual property and gives you the peace of mind to focus on growing your business.

Tip # 3

Obtain Legal Counsel

Finally, Benjamin emphasizes the importance of **obtaining legal counsel**.

Navigating copyright and patent law can be complex, so seeking the guidance of an experienced attorney is crucial. Benjamin encourages entrepreneurs to reach out for professional help, even if it means seeking pro bono services. "Don't be afraid to reach out to an attorney," he advises.

Many resources are available, including state bar associations' referral services and pro bono legal clinics, to help guide you through the process. While hiring an attorney may feel intimidating or costly, Benjamin assures entrepreneurs that this investment in professional guidance is well worth it for protecting their business assets.

Example

Protecting the Big Idea: One Entrepreneur's Journey from Concept to Copyright

A creative entrepreneur had finally hit on an idea they knew was special — a unique product concept that blended innovation with real market demand. But as excitement grew, so did a quiet fear: What if someone else takes this before I make it real? They weren't sure where to start, but they knew protecting their idea had to become a priority.

That realization led to **Tip #1: Keep Diligent Notes**. Instead of relying on memory or scattered files, they began keeping organized records of every draft, diagram, and development date. Whether jotting ideas in a bound notebook or uploading updates to a cloud folder with timestamps, they treated their creative process like it mattered — because it did. These notes became a living archive that proved ownership and tracked progress. More importantly, they gave the entrepreneur confidence that they could defend their work if needed.

With records in place, they turned to **Tip #2: File Early**. They learned about the "first-to-file" principle and how waiting too long could cost them their rights. Rather than overthinking it, they filed a provisional patent to hold their spot while finalizing the full version. For creative works, they registered copyrights as soon as their drafts were complete. Early filing didn't just protect them legally — it gave them peace of mind to start pitching and producing without hesitation.

Lastly, they took the bold but necessary step of following **Tip #3: Obtain Legal Counsel**. Though nervous about the cost, they reached out to a small business legal clinic and found free guidance through a nonprofit. An attorney helped them clean up documentation, refine their filings, and understand what protections were realistic. Instead of navigating IP law alone, they now had an expert in their corner.

Today, that entrepreneur's idea is not only protected — it's thriving in the marketplace. And while the journey to secure their intellectual property wasn't always easy, it was foundational.

Because in business, having a great idea is only half the battle. Protecting it? That's what turns potential into power.

Questions and Key Takeaways

Key Takeaways from Benjamin Dach:

- Keep organized and diligent notes on your ideas and when they were conceived.
- File your copyrights and patents early to ensure protection and prevent others from claiming your work.
- Don't hesitate to seek legal counsel and take advantage of pro bono services if necessary.

Food for Thought

- What methods do you use to document and organize your ideas to establish clear ownership and development timelines?
- Why is it important to file for intellectual property protection early, and what challenges can arise if you delay?
- How can entrepreneurs access affordable legal support, and what benefits have you seen from consulting with legal experts early in the process?

Bio

Guest Expert - Benjamin Dach, Ph.D., J.D.

Benjamin Dach is a leading intellectual property attorney based in Miami, Florida, specializing in patent, trademark, and copyright law. With a unique combination of technical expertise and legal acumen, Dr. Dach has helped clients secure and protect intellectual property assets worth over $10 billion throughout his career.

Dr. Dach earned his Ph.D. in engineering before pursuing his legal education at Fordham University School of Law, where he received his J.D. in 2017. This dual background enables him to understand both the technical complexities of innovations and the legal strategies needed to protect them effectively.

Admitted to practice in Florida, New York, New Jersey, and before the United States Patent and Trademark Office, Dr. Dach represents clients ranging from individual inventors to Fortune 500 companies. His practice encompasses patent prosecution, trademark registration, copyright protection, IP due diligence, and complex intellectual property litigation.

Recognized as a Rising Star in Law for 2023, Dr. Dach is known for his strategic approach to IP protection and his ability to translate complex legal concepts into actionable business strategies. He frequently speaks at industry conferences and provides pro bono services to support emerging entrepreneurs and startups.

Dr. Dach's philosophy centers on proactive protection: helping clients identify, document, and secure their intellectual property assets before problems arise, rather than reacting to disputes after they develop.

Chapter 26: The Greatest Risk to You and Your Business

Guest Expert: Julwel Kenney, Ph.D.

"Prepare today so your business can survive tomorrow."
— Julwel Kenney, Ph.D.

Entrepreneurs often focus on growth, but real success also means being ready for the unexpected. Dr. Julwel Kenney draws from deep personal experience to stress the importance of protecting yourself and your business from life's inevitable curveballs. In this chapter, she shares how building a financial cushion, securing proper insurance, and considering the right business partnerships can shield your business and your life from devastating setbacks.

Tip #1

Build a Financial Safety Net

One of the most critical steps entrepreneurs can take is establishing an emergency fund. Dr. Kenney emphasizes saving at least six months' worth of personal living and business operating expenses. Even small, consistent contributions, $10, $20, or $50 at a time, can add up significantly over the years. She shares, "If I hadn't had savings when I got hurt, we would have been in serious trouble." This financial buffer offers security when unexpected challenges arise, giving you the flexibility to recover without losing everything you've built.

Tip #2

Obtain Adequate Insurance Coverage

Dr. Kenney underscores that insurance is an investment in your peace of mind. Comprehensive health insurance, including hospitalization and specialist care, is crucial, especially for single entrepreneurs who might not have other safety nets. She also highlights the importance of disability insurance, recommending policies that cover both short- and long-term needs. "Look for affordable options," she advises, "and don't forget workers' compensation insurance. It's more accessible than many realize and can provide critical protection at a relatively low monthly cost."

Tip # 3

Consider a Trusted Business Partner

Having a reliable partner can help share the burdens of entrepreneurship, but Dr. Kenney warns that choosing the right person is vital. She encourages entrepreneurs to pray, reflect, and carefully assess potential partners, ensuring they align in vision, values, and work ethic. "The right partner can help you build and grow safely," she says, "but the wrong one can cause more harm than good." It's a decision that should never be rushed.

Example

Prepared to Prevail: One Entrepreneur's Plan for the Unexpected

For years, an independent business owner was laser-focused on growth, landing clients, launching products, and building momentum. But everything changed the moment a personal health crisis hit. Business slowed to a crawl, bills piled up, and the pressure mounted. That's when they realized: success isn't just about growth; it's also about protection.

Thankfully, they had already taken **Tip #1: Build a Financial Safety Net** to heart. Even before trouble struck, they made a habit of setting aside small amounts from each paycheck, $25 here, $50 there. Over time, those deposits added up to a reserve fund that covered six months of living and business expenses. That cushion became a lifeline, allowing them to stay afloat, cover bills, and focus on recovery without panic. The peace of mind it provided was worth every dollar saved.

But it wasn't just savings that kept things stable; it was also **Tip #2: Obtain Adequate Insurance Coverage**. They had secured a comprehensive health insurance plan that included hospital and specialist coverage, as well as a disability policy that kicked in when they couldn't work. That foresight meant they didn't have to deplete their savings or shut down operations entirely. Even workers' comp, often overlooked by solo entrepreneurs, proved valuable when a subcontractor was injured on-site. The right coverage turned potential catastrophe into a manageable detour.

Looking ahead, they began thinking more strategically, which led to **Tip #3: Consider a Trusted Business Partner**. Running a business solo had its perks, but the experience taught them the importance of not going alone. They didn't rush the process. Instead, they evaluated their network, clarified their values, and waited for the right fit. Eventually, they found someone who complemented their skills, shared their vision, and could step in when needed. Together, they built a stronger, more resilient foundation.

This entrepreneur's journey is a reminder that the best way to weather life's storms is to prepare before they hit. With a safety net, smart insurance, and a solid support system, they didn't just survive a crisis; they came back wiser, stronger, and ready for whatever came next.

Questions and Key Takeaways

Key Takeaways from Julwel Kenney, Ph.D.:

- Build a financial safety net to cover at least six months of expenses.
- Obtain comprehensive insurance coverage, including health, disability, and workers' compensation.
- Carefully select a business partner who shares your values and vision.

Food for Thought

- What steps can small business owners take to build a financial cushion that can sustain them through unexpected challenges?
- How do you determine the right types and levels of insurance coverage needed to protect both yourself and your business?
- What qualities or conversations should entrepreneurs prioritize when choosing a business partner to ensure long-term alignment and trust?

Bio

Guest Expert - Julwel Kenney, Ph.D.

Dr. Julwel Kenney's leadership and strategic capabilities are evident in her role as the CEO and Transformation Doctor at JK Personal & Professional Development LLC. (JKPPD) since 2011. JKPPD is a testament to her commitment to collaborating with organizations and individuals to enhance performance, productivity, profitability, and retention through effective training, coaching, and change management strategies. Her personal journey, marked by the pursuit of academic excellence, including a Ph.D. in Training & Performance Improvement, MS in Organizational Leadership, and MBA in HR, is a testament to her resilience and determination. Dr. Kenney is also the best-selling author of 4 books on leadership and executive coaching, one of which was co-authored by Dr. Steven Covey, Dr. John Gray, and Les Brown. Her guiding philosophy, "Winners Never Quit, and Quitters Never Win", resonates with her belief that "It is Your Time, Your Turn, Your Season to Achieve the Greatness in You!"

Chapter 27: How To Make a Sustainable Business Model

Guest Expert: Terry Trayvick

"Fix the core first, then focus on growth." — Terry Trayvick

Terry Trayvick is an experienced business leader who emphasizes that long-term success starts with a strong foundation. In his session, he outlines the critical steps to building a sustainable business model that not only grows but endures. His straightforward three-point strategy offers entrepreneurs a clear roadmap for building resilient, profitable businesses.

Tip #1

Fix the Core Business First

Terry's first rule is simple but powerful: **before thinking about growth, fix your core operations**. "Plug up the leaky holes," he says. Before investing energy into acquiring new customers or expanding offerings, business owners must ensure that the systems supporting their current customers are strong. A poorly run core business is like a leaky bucket; no matter how much new business you pour in, you'll lose what you already have if you don't fix the foundation.

Tip #2

Choose and Commit to a Growth Path

Once the core is strong, it's time to **determine your growth path**. According to Terry, there are two primary ways to grow:

- Take your existing product or service to a broader audience.
- Offer new products or services to your existing customer base.

Trying to do both at once spreads your resources too thin. "Pick one path, focus your resources, and stick to it," Terry advises. Clear focus enables more effective marketing, operations, and customer service strategies tailored to your chosen direction.

Tip # 3

Compete Strategically

Businesses can't compete on everything at once. Terry encourages entrepreneurs to **choose what they want to compete on**, whether that's price, quality, customer service, innovation, or something else, and work relentlessly to become the best at it. Distinguishing yourself from competitors through a clearly defined advantage helps build customer loyalty and strengthens your brand over time.

Example

From Chaos to Clarity: A Small Business Turnaround

A few years ago, a small family-owned HVAC company was struggling despite steady demand. Customers were leaving negative reviews, employees felt burned out, and profits were on the decline. Yet the owner remained focused on generating new leads, convinced that growth was the key to success.

But pouring more business into a broken system only made things worse.

That's where **Tip #1: Fix the Core Business First** comes into play. The company paused its expansion plans to conduct a thorough review of internal operations. They discovered billing inconsistencies, delayed response times, and poor communication across teams, all of which were quietly driving customers away. By streamlining their scheduling system, retraining staff, and implementing a CRM tool to manage workflows and communication, they created a much smoother customer experience. As service quality improved, so did customer satisfaction and retention.

With the core stabilized, the business turned its attention to growth. Rather than try to do everything at once, they followed **Tip #2: Choose and Commit to a Growth Path**. They opted to expand into new geographic markets using their existing service model instead of adding new services. This focused approach allowed them to concentrate marketing and sales efforts in a way that maximized results, ultimately increasing revenue by over 40% in just one year.

Finally, they applied **Tip #3: Compete Strategically**. Recognizing that they couldn't win on price alone, the company chose to compete on reliability and customer service. They built their brand around the promise of "on-time service, guaranteed", and backed it up with real performance. That clear positioning set them apart in a crowded industry and helped build strong customer loyalty.

The result wasn't just a turnaround; it was a foundation for sustainable growth. This story is a clear reminder that business growth doesn't start with expansion. It starts by fixing what's broken, making smart choices about where to grow, and standing out for the right reasons.

Questions and Key Takeaways

Key Takeaways from Terry Trayvick:

- Repair and strengthen your core operations before seeking growth.
- Choose one clear growth strategy and commit to it.
- Decide what your business will compete on and strive to be the best at it.

Food for Thought

- What core areas of your business need to be stabilized or improved before you can confidently pursue growth?
- How do you determine the most effective growth strategy for your business, and what does commitment to that path look like in practice?
- What unique value or competitive edge does your business offer, and how are you working to lead in that specific area?

Bio

Guest Expert - Terry Trayvick

Terry Trayvick has over 30 years of business experience with a strong track record of leading organizations to outstanding results.

As CEO of Level Five Consulting, he brings world-class management tools and processes to companies to take them from good to great.

Section #3

Financing Growth

"Where Will I Find the Money," the key theme in chapter 4 of my first book *Running Your Small Business Like A Pro*. Unfortunately, most business owners seeking to access capital do not qualify for or deserve financing at the point they are seeking it because they are unprepared. I share with them my proven strategy for helping them to access more capital with the best terms, faster and easier.

They must P.R.A.Y. for financing, not necessarily on their knees, but that can't hurt. My P.R.A.Y. system consists of the following steps...

- **PREPARE** yourself and Your Business
- **RESEARCH** financing types and sources
- **ASSEMBLE** the necessary documents

- **YIELD** during the due diligence and the underwriting process

Without following my P.R.A.Y. system, you significantly reduce your potential to access capital or result in less optimal financing, which can hurt or restrict your business flexibility in the future.

Fortunately, the experts in this book have proven expertise and significant experience with small business financing under various circumstances. That's what makes this section so valuable and relevant for you.

Chapter 28: How to Finance Your Contracts

Guest Expert: Ervin Hughes Jr.

"Build business credit, expand your offerings, and always bid profitably." — Ervin Hughes Jr.

Ervin Hughes Jr. is an expert in helping businesses secure and finance government and private sector contracts. In this chapter, he outlines three essential strategies every entrepreneur must master to successfully finance their contracts and grow sustainably. His advice offers a clear and actionable blueprint for building a stronger, more profitable business.

Tip #1

Build Business Credit

The first critical step, according to Ervin, is establishing and strengthening your business credit. "You have to have it. You must build it. It must be built. It's a process," he emphasizes. Solid business credit not only positions your company to win contracts but also helps you access the funding needed to perform on those contracts confidently. Without it, scaling and seizing bigger opportunities becomes nearly impossible.

Tip #2

Expand Offerings Within Your Industry

Ervin encourages entrepreneurs to think bigger by offering both goods and services related to their core business. "If you're a janitorial service, why aren't you selling janitorial supplies?" he asks. By diversifying what you offer within your niche, you create multiple streams of revenue, make yourself more valuable to clients, and open the door to larger, more lucrative contracts.

Tip # 3

Always Bid Profitably

Finally, profitability must remain at the forefront when pursuing contracts. Ervin stresses the importance of having a well-thought-out pricing strategy. "Make sure you're profitable when you're going after contract opportunities," he warns. Without a strategic approach to pricing, businesses can win work that ultimately drains resources rather than grows revenue. Being smart about your bids protects your margins and ensures your company's long-term success.

Example

From Small Jobs to Government Contracts: One Entrepreneur's Strategic Climb

A few years ago, a small business owner in the cleaning industry was stuck in a cycle of short-term gigs and razor-thin margins. She knew she was capable of handling bigger clients and government contracts, but every attempt to scale felt out of reach. The opportunities were there, but she couldn't quite break through.

Everything started to shift when she followed **Tip #1: Build Business Credit**. Instead of using her personal credit to float business expenses, she took intentional steps to establish a strong business credit profile. She opened a business bank account, registered with DUNS, and strategically used vendor accounts to build history. "It didn't happen overnight," she admitted, "but once my business credit was in place, I could finally access the capital I needed to go after larger contracts." That foundation gave her the confidence and capacity to start bidding on bigger opportunities.

With credit in place, she turned to **Tip #2: Expand Offerings Within Your Industry**. She realized that clients who trusted her cleaning services were also sourcing janitorial supplies elsewhere. So, she began offering eco-friendly cleaning products as part of her proposals. This small pivot added a new revenue stream, positioned her as a one-stop solution, and made her bids more attractive. Over time, it also helped her land multi-year contracts with school districts and municipalities.

But her biggest breakthrough came from **Tip #3: Always Bid Profitably**. Early on, she had made the mistake of underbidding just to win contracts, only to find herself scrambling to meet expectations without making a dime. This time, she developed a clear pricing structure that factored in labor, materials, logistics, and a sustainable profit margin. "It's not just about getting the contract," she said. "It's about growing without going broke."

Today, that once-struggling entrepreneur manages a thriving team, has multiple service contracts in place, and continues to grow with confidence. Her story proves that with strong business credit, smart expansion, and disciplined pricing, small businesses can position themselves for big success, not just by working harder, but by working smarter.

If your company does not get paid at the point of sale and your government or corporate customers require you to deliver your products or complete your work and then invoice them and await payment to be made at some point in the future, then your company is extending credit to your customers. If your company is extending credit, then your company is a creditor. If your company is a creditor, are you extending credit to your customers without checking their credit first? Most business owners do know this, but if you're an awarded government contractor, did you know that you can finance your contracts by leveraging the full faith and credit of your government agency or large corporate customers to secure a "debt-free" receivable-based credit line? If you didn't know this, don't worry, most people don't know this.

Many business owners have been conditioned to believe that "cash is king." This is true if you're buying tires or groceries, but not so if you are a small business with a contract to provide goods or services. Why? Because cash is cash. It does not renew. When cash is gone. It's gone. Credit, on the other hand, is a renewable instrument. Meaning that you can use credit, then repay it, and use it again. This is called revolving credit. You can use credit to cover your expenses for inventory, materials, equipment, and supplies to fulfill your obligations under a contract, and then when you invoice your creditworthy customers, you can draw cash now instead of waiting 30, 60, or 90 days to be paid. Here's a pro tip: if you sell on credit, then you must buy on credit. If you sell on credit and buy on cash, it will drain your bank account, cause cash flow problems, and inhibit your company's ability to grow its revenue and profits.

Questions and Key Takeaways

Key Takeaways from Ervin Hughes Jr.:

- Establish and grow strong business credit to access larger contract opportunities.
- Expand into related goods and services within your industry for multiple revenue streams.
- Never use credit to pay bills – use credit to make money.

Food for Thought

- What steps can a small business take to build strong business credit, and how does it impact their ability to win larger contracts?
- How can businesses identify complementary products or services that align with their core offering and open new revenue streams?
- What factors should you consider when developing a pricing strategy that balances competitiveness with profitability?

Bio

Guest Expert - Ervin Hughes Jr.

Ervin Hughes, Jr., has diverse work experience spanning several industries. Ervin is currently serving as the President of American Credit Assurance, LLC, a minority-owned purchase order finance company. Prior to this, they held the position of Managing Director at Rainstar Capital Group. Ervin also has experience in academia, working as an Adjunct Professor at Houston Community College and a Senior Mentor at the University of Houston-Bauer School of Business. Additionally, they have held executive roles, including Chief Executive Officer at New Covenant Capital Corporation and Covenant Capital Corporation. Ervin has also worked as a Commercial Banker at Central Bank, where they designed and implemented contract finance solutions for small business customers. Ervin is an active member of the Association for Corporate Growth Houston.

Chapter 29: Secrets to Successfully Buy or Sell a Business

Guest Expert: Richard Parker

"Buying a business is very doable for the average person — and success depends on staying realistic." — Richard Parker

Richard Parker is one of the top experts in the world when it comes to buying and selling businesses. With decades of experience and tens of thousands of clients, he knows exactly what separates successful deals from frustrating failures. In this chapter, Richard shares simple but crucial principles that every entrepreneur should understand, whether they are planning to buy or sell a business.

Tip #1

Buying a Business Is More Achievable Than You Think

Many people wrongly believe that buying a business is only for the wealthy or big corporations. Richard debunks this myth: "Buying a business is very doable for the average individual." He emphasizes that with creative options like seller financing, which 91% of his clients have used successfully, everyday entrepreneurs can step into business ownership. If you have even a hint of entrepreneurial spirit, you owe it to yourself to explore buying instead of building from scratch.

Tip #2

Keep the End Goal in Mind

Whether you're buying or selling, it's easy to get bogged down in the small stuff. Richard warns entrepreneurs not to lose sight of the bigger picture. "People get so immersed and emotional that they focus on the wrong things," he says. The solution? Focus on building a good relationship between buyer and seller. Meaningful conversations and mutual respect will help both sides avoid unnecessary battles and keep the deal moving forward toward a successful close.

Tip # 3

Stay Realistic Throughout the Process

One of the biggest pitfalls Richard sees is people having unrealistic expectations, about valuations, deal structures, or timelines. "Start breathing oxygen from this planet," he advises bluntly. Ignore the internet noise about overnight business buys and too-good-to-be-true deals. Real success comes from maintaining fairness, reasonableness, and being grounded in what's possible.

Example

From Dreamer to Deal-Maker: How One Entrepreneur Bought Her First Business

For years, Louise, a sales professional, dreamed of owning her own business. She loved the idea of being her own boss but felt overwhelmed by the idea of building something from scratch. With no tech startup idea, no investors, and a modest savings account, she assumed entrepreneurship just wasn't in the cards.

That changed when she discovered **Tip #1: Buying a Business Is More Achievable Than You Think**. At a local business seminar, she heard Richard explain how average individuals, not just wealthy people, were becoming business owners through creative deal structures, such as seller financing. Skeptical but intrigued, she explored listings for small businesses and reached out to owners. To her surprise, several were open to flexible terms, including one seller who offered to finance 70% of the deal himself. "That was my lightbulb moment," she recalls. "Buying a business wasn't out of reach. I just hadn't known how to find them or what to ask."

As the deal progressed, she leaned on **Tip #2: Keep the End Goal in Mind**. There were hiccups, financial reviews, negotiation stress, and some heated discussions about valuation and transition timelines. But she remembered Richard's advice: "*build the relationship, not just the deal*". She focused on staying respectful and communicative with the seller, who had built the business over 20 years and cared deeply about its future. That mutual trust smoothed the way and helped them find common ground on every challenge.

Of course, she also had to apply **Tip #3: Stay Realistic Throughout the Process**. At first, she hoped for a perfect turnkey business that would instantly generate six figures. "I had to let go of the fantasy," she admits. Richard's blunt reminder, "*Start breathing oxygen from this planet*", helped her temper her expectations. She focused on what was achievable, understanding there's no such thing as a 'perfect' business, and that mindset kept her grounded through all the steps in the business-buying process.

Today, she owns a thriving commercial cleaning company with steady clients, double-digit growth, four additional locations, and a growing team. She didn't invent something new or raise venture capital; she bought a good existing business at a great price and terms and made it flourish on her own. Her journey proves that with the right mindset, know-how, relationship building, and realism, business ownership is closer than most people think.

Questions and Key Takeaways

Key Takeaways from Richard Parker:

- Buying a business is achievable for everyday people, especially with tools like seller financing.
- Focus on the bigger goal and maintain a good relationship with the other party.
- Stay realistic about valuations, timelines, and expectations for a smooth deal.

Food for Thought

- What makes seller financing an accessible option for aspiring business owners, and how can someone get started with it?
- How can maintaining a positive relationship with the seller or partner help facilitate a smoother and more successful business deal?
- What are some common misconceptions about buying a business, and how can staying grounded in realistic expectations lead to better outcomes?

Bio

Guest Expert - Richard Parker

RICHARD PARKER has been helping people achieve their dreams of owning a business for over 30 years. His 'How To Buy A Good Business At A Great Price' program has sold over 100,000 copies in more than 80 countries.

He was a partner with Ray Dalio and the Dalio family office for four years in an investment firm that was set up for Richard to mentor one of Ray's sons in the art of buying businesses.

He has personally purchased 13 of his own companies, plus one co-investment, with purchase prices ranging from $50,000 to over $200 million.

Richard has appeared in Forbes, The New York Times, TheStreet.com, Entrepreneur Magazine, Inc., and has more than 200 published articles to his credit.

Chapter 30: The Secret to Raising Capital for an Acquisition

Guest Expert: Kevin Bibelhausen

"Acquisition growth isn't just for Wall Street — it's a smart, accessible path for small business owners too."
— Kevin Bibelhausen

Kevin Bibelhausen is a finance expert who brings Wall Street strategies to small and mid-sized business owners. In this chapter, he demystifies the process of raising capital to acquire another business and explains why acquisition is one of the most effective ways to scale faster without starting from scratch. His practical, down-to-earth advice reminds entrepreneurs that success is about mindset, education, and making informed decisions.

Tip #1

Acquisition Is a Powerful Growth Hack

Growing your business organically through marketing and sales is great, but acquiring another business can be a game-changer. Kevin explains that acquisitions allow you to add complementary products or services without starting from zero. "You can jump in with a lot of the hard part already done," he says. For entrepreneurs looking to scale quickly and diversify, acquisition is a highly strategic lever to pull.

Tip #2

It's More Accessible Than You Think

Many small business owners assume acquisitions are too complex or out of reach. Kevin emphasizes that this isn't true: "It's not as complicated as people make it seem." Traditional finance professionals might cloud the process in jargon, but basic acquisition strategies are doable for everyday entrepreneurs. Tools like SBA loans and the growing number of accessible investment funds make it easier than ever to finance a business purchase without needing millions in the bank.

Tip # 3

Tap into the Wealth of Resources

If you want to grow via acquisition, your network and knowledge will be your biggest assets. Kevin encourages entrepreneurs to reach out, ask questions, and learn from credible sources — not from "no-money-down" hype artists. Resources on LinkedIn, Twitter, and even direct mentorship can give you practical guidance. "Put yourself out there, build your network, and educate yourself," Kevin advises. "If you've built a business from scratch, you already have what it takes."

Example

In January 2022, I decided to stop waiting and start searching. I'd thought about buying a business for years, but a Covid-related health scare made the opportunity cost of inaction too high to ignore. Within 12 months, I had raised $800,000 from accredited investors I didn't previously know, completely cold, and closed on a $7.8M acquisition.

The deal: a 20-year-old wholesale textile business doing nearly $10 million in annual sales. I saw operational upside, sticky customer relationships, and margin headroom. We structured it with an SBA 7(a) loan, a seller's note, and my investor equity round. No fancy firm. No inherited deal flow. Just a sharp thesis, a clean pitch, and relentless follow-up.

The biggest unlock. Investors are open to backing first-time buyers if you make it easy for them to say yes. I didn't have a traditional finance pedigree. What I did have was a clear story, a realistic model, and the ability to communicate both with urgency and transparency. That credibility, combined with a well-structured deal, was enough.

That first acquisition changed everything. I now run the company as its president while building a fund to back other acquisition entrepreneurs. Buying a business isn't reserved for Wall Street. If you've built something from scratch before, you already have the grit and intuition needed to operate something proven. Add capital, and you've got a flywheel.

Questions and Key Takeaways

Key Takeaways from Kevin Bibelhausen:

- Acquisition is a fast-track way to grow by adding complementary services without starting from scratch.
- Financing an acquisition is more accessible than many entrepreneurs realize, thanks to programs like SBA loans.
- A strong network and credible resources are essential to learning the right way to succeed.

Food for Thought

- How can acquiring an existing business help accelerate growth and expand your service offerings more efficiently than building from the ground up?
- What financing options are available to entrepreneurs looking to acquire a business, and how can they navigate those opportunities effectively?
- How has your network or access to expert resources influenced your ability to make smart acquisition or business decisions?

Bio

Guest Expert - Kevin Bibelhausen

It is remarkable how quickly someone can transform their life when they buy a business. Kevin Bibelhausen suffered a Covid-related health scare that caused him to re-evaluate things. He'd flirted with buying a business before, but after this scare, he got serious about it. Today, just 1 year later, Kevin raised $800k from investors (that he did not already know) to buy a business valued at almost $8 million. He is now the owner & president of a 20-year-old wholesale fabrics business that generates almost $10 million in annual sales, in addition to being the general partner in a fund that invests in other search engine deals himself. Not bad for a year of work.

Chapter 31: Growth and Profit: Solving the Capacity Conundrum

Guest Expert: Scott Springer

"Strategy, bottleneck-busting, and positive communication drive sustainable growth and profit." — Scott Springer

Scott Springer, a leader in operational excellence and business transformation, has coached manufacturers and growth companies by focusing on capacity, the hidden engine that drives (or limits) every business's speed and profit. His three-pronged approach, developing a long-term strategy, proactively identifying and fixing bottlenecks, and leading with encouraging communication, helps companies scale faster by addressing what holds them back.

Tip #1

Build a Strategy for Growth and Culture

Scott insists that true success starts with looking years ahead. Your strategy should define how much you'll produce, what markets you'll serve, and, crucially, what kind of organizational culture you want. He stresses that culture is built over time, not overnight, and should be woven into every strategic discussion. Include capacity planning directly in your big-picture vision so you're always anticipating the next phase of growth.

Tip #2

Find and Fix Your Bottlenecks

Every business has a bottleneck, whether it's a slow machine, a short-staffed team, a limited supplier, or a jammed sales process. Scott urges leaders to identify these pinch points, understand their capacity limits, and systematically solve (or outgrow) them. And when you fix one, plan for the next, because another will always appear as you scale. Be relentless and proactive in bottleneck-busting to keep your growth on track.

Tip # 3

Communicate Relentlessly and Positively

Nothing breaks down operations faster than poor communication. Scott advocates for leadership at every level to engage all employees, share progress, and foster a positive environment. "Half the job of being a leader is being a cheerleader," Scott says.

He recommends that for every critique, offer 10 pieces of positive feedback. This builds morale and keeps teams focused and motivated as they tackle operational challenges together.

Example

Tip #1: Build a Strategy for Growth and Culture

A food manufacturing company mapped out a three-year plan that didn't just cover revenue targets but also detailed investments in staff training and the deliberate creation of a "continuous improvement" culture. This clarity helped align big goals with daily actions.

Tip #2: Find and Fix Your Bottlenecks

While reviewing the plan, the plant manager identified the slowest piece of equipment in the production line, limiting all output. By investing in an upgrade and then shifting focus to the next emerging bottleneck (a packaging supply delay), the team stayed ahead of demand and doubled throughput within 18 months.

Tip #3: Communicate Relentlessly and Positively

Weekly "all hands" meetings kept every staff member (from VPs to line workers) informed on performance, upcoming changes, and who was exceeding expectations. Leaders made it a standard practice to recognize individual wins before discussing problems, creating a culture where employees were eager to solve issues and share their solutions.

Questions and Key Takeaways

Key Takeaways from Scott Springer:

- Develop a long-term strategy that covers growth, capacity, and the culture you want to build.
- Continually seek out and solve the next biggest bottleneck holding back your business.
- Use frequent, positive communication to engage your entire team and fuel momentum through change.

Food for Thought

- Do you have a three-year capacity and culture strategy, or is your focus limited to the next quarter?
- Where's your biggest bottleneck right now, and what's your plan to fix it and predict the next one?
- How often do you recognize your team's wins versus pointing out shortcomings?

Bio

Guest Expert - Scott Springer

Scott Springer is an accomplished executive consultant and business leader recognized for cultivating and executing high-growth strategies across diverse industries.

He is recognized for engineering operational processes to revitalize underperforming organizations, optimizing productivity, safety, and long-term profitability through the application of Lean methodologies and strategic planning.

Regarded as a change agent, Scott excels in organizational development, revenue growth, and team building, with expertise spanning operational improvement, business market penetration, and mergers and acquisitions.

Chapter 32: Getting Venture Financing for a Venture

Guest Expert: Calvin Reed

"A dream without a plan is wishful thinking; resources, questions, and determination are what bring your venture to life." — Calvin Reed

Calvin Reed, a veteran in real estate, urban development, and venture creation, knows firsthand that accessing capital for your dream project is rarely a straight line. In this chapter, he shares what separates those who win at the fundraising game from those who just wish: a bulletproof plan, a relentless curiosity, and unwavering commitment.

Tip #1

Have a Solid Business Plan

Calvin says the foundation for landing any investment is a robust, well-thought-out business plan. It's not just a checklist item for grants or VCs, it's a statement of vision, credibility, and commitment. Potential backers want to know you've mapped out your market, milestones, team, and numbers, and that you understand your own roadmap backward and forward.

Tip #2

Fearlessly Use Every Resource and Ask Every Question

Too many entrepreneurs let pride, fear, or hesitation keep them from asking for help. Calvin's advice: ask questions and tap every available resource, including mentors, industry contacts, past investors, online forums, AI tools, and even your competitors. Insight and funding flow to those who are resourceful, courageous, and always willing to seek, adapt, and learn.

Tip # 3

Make Determination Your Daily Habit

Perhaps Calvin's strongest message: grit trumps all. Getting a "no" from an investor isn't failure; it's feedback for your next pitch. Stay committed, even after setbacks, long waits, or changes in direction. The founders who persist are those who redefine the possible and make it through to launch, scale, and have an impact.

Example

Tip #1: Have a Solid Business Plan

Calvin once needed to raise seed capital for a cable company. More than any elevator pitch, it was a crisp, comprehensive business plan, covering product, numbers, and strategy, that secured the first "yes" from a fund. Knowing his plan cold made him credible in every conversation thereafter.

Tip #2: Fearlessly Use Every Resource and Ask Every Question

Out of his network, Calvin found mentors and subject-matter experts for each funding stage, constantly asking: "What do I not know? What will help my business stand out?" He emailed industry veterans, found government programs, and joined VC office hours. Asking "why not me?" turned missed opportunities into learning and improved proposals.

Tip #3: Make Determination Your Daily Habit

Calvin's venture faced rejection after rejection, but each "no" became a roadmap for his next approach. From reworking his pitch after investor feedback to pivoting his offering, it was daily determination and a willingness to start over that finally brought success (and future investors) to the table.

Questions and Key Takeaways

Key Takeaways from Calvin Reed:

- A strong business plan is your most persuasive tool. Prepare it, master it, and let it speak for you.
- Every question you ask and every resource you seek out draws you closer to the funds and wisdom you need.
- Determination and resilience turn "no" into "not yet", stick to your vision and adapt along the way.

Food for Thought

- When was the last time you updated or truly "owned" your own business plan from top to bottom?
- Which mentors, experts, or resources are you under-leveraging right now?
- How do you keep your own drive alive after facing setbacks in your fundraising or business journey?

Bio

Guest Expert - Calvin Reed

Calvin Reed is an accomplished entrepreneur, author, and financial educator dedicated to helping others achieve financial success and personal growth. He is the founder of Platinum Financial Resources, Inc., and Executive Vice President of New Africa Development Corporation in Newark, NJ.

Calvin co-founded Connection Communications Corporation, which was awarded Newark, New Jersey's initial cable franchise in 1978. He served as the Vice-President for Marketing and Corporate Development from 1978 until the company was sold in 1986. The company also obtained cable franchises for South Orange, Jersey City, and twenty-two locations in South Carolina.

Calvin graduated from Lincoln University with studies in English Literature and economics. He participated in a semester abroad program, studying in Belgium, England, France, and Spain, and later attended the University of Denver's Publishing Institute.

Chapter 33: Secrets to Raising Capital in Any Environment

Guest Expert: Dr. Randal Pinkett

"Seek significance, not just success." — Dr. Randal Pinkett

Raising capital demands more than just having a great idea or polished financials. It requires clarity of purpose, an entrepreneurial mindset, and a focus beyond personal gain. Dr. Randal Pinkett, entrepreneur, scholar, and CEO of BCT Partners, shares timeless principles that can guide anyone seeking to stand out and attract the right support.

Tip #1

Find Your Ikigai — Your Meaning

The first, and perhaps most powerful, step is to **discover your Ikigai** — a Japanese concept meaning "reason for being."

Ikigai lies at the intersection of four key questions:

- What do you love to do?
- What are you good at doing?
- What does the world need?
- What can you get paid to do?

When you find the alignment between passion, skill, market need, and financial viability, you operate from a position of authentic purpose. Investors and partners are drawn to people who know their "why" and live it clearly.

(Tip: Google "Ikigai diagram" to visualize this powerful concept.)

Tip #2

Think Like an Entrepreneur

You don't need to own a business to **think like an entrepreneur**.

Entrepreneurial thinking, *creativity, resourcefulness, courage, resilience, and passion* are now essential for everyone, whether you're raising capital, leading a team, or managing a career.

Embracing this mindset enables you to adapt to challenges, identify opportunities, and demonstrate the tenacity that investors and stakeholders respect. No matter what your field, adopting entrepreneurial thinking can be your edge in a fast-changing world.

Tip # 3

Seek Significance, Not Just Success

Finally, Randall urges us to **shift from seeking success to seeking significance**.

Success is about what you do for yourself. Significance is about what you do for others.

Be a **Go-Giver**, not just a Go-Getter.

Prioritize relationships, service, and creating impact over mere transactions. When you genuinely add value to others, you naturally attract goodwill, partnership, and yes, investment.

Those who focus on making a difference often find that financial rewards follow naturally.

Example

From Confused to Connected: A Journey Through Purpose, Mindset, and Meaning

A few years ago, a corporate project manager found herself at a crossroads. On paper, she was thriving, with a six-figure salary, an impressive title, and steady promotions. But beneath the surface, she felt adrift. It wasn't a burnout. It was a misalignment. She had built a successful career but couldn't shake the feeling that she wasn't doing what she was meant to do.

Everything began to shift when she encountered **Tip #1: Find Your Ikigai**, the Japanese concept that combines what you love, what you're good at, what the world needs, and what you can get paid to do. As she reflected deeply on her passions, strengths, and core values, a new vision began to emerge. She realized her real joy came from wellness, mentorship, and helping others navigate personal transformation.

Instead of quitting her job overnight, she began a side project: a wellness coaching platform for corporate professionals facing burnout. This move wasn't just about a new business; it was about reconnecting with her purpose in a real, grounded way.

As her platform took shape, she embraced **Tip #2: Think Like an Entrepreneur**. Though she had no background in business, she started to act like a founder. She identified the challenges her peers faced, tested content through webinars, and built an audience from scratch. She even collaborated with her employer to pilot an internal wellness coaching program, an initiative that gained even more relevance during the pandemic.

This shift in mindset, from employee to innovator, helped her stand out. No longer just a manager of projects, she became a thought leader with timely solutions. Her ideas weren't just welcomed; they were sought out.

But the most profound transformation came when she adopted **Tip #3: Seek Significance, Not Just Success**. Rather than chasing accolades or income, she focused on the impact she could make. She offered free sessions to healthcare workers, partnered with nonprofits, and centered her efforts around service, not sales.

And as often happens when purpose meets generosity, doors begin to open. Speaking opportunities, media coverage, and aligned investors followed. Within two years, she transitioned into full-time entrepreneurship, not because she was chasing success, but because she had built something meaningful.

Her story is a reminder that the most powerful journeys don't always start with quitting a job or launching a business. Sometimes, they begin with an honest look inward. By discovering her Ikigai, embracing an entrepreneurial mindset, and leading with service, she moved from confusion to clarity and built a life that made a difference.

Questions and Key Takeaways

Key Takeaways from Dr. Randal Pinkett:

- Discover your Ikigai, align passion, skill, need, and opportunity.
- Adopt entrepreneurial thinking, be creative, resilient, and courageous.
- Focus on significance, prioritize service to others over personal gain.

Food for Thought

- How can discovering your Ikigai help you align your career or business path with what truly drives you, and how do you balance passion, skill, need, and opportunity?
- What are some ways to cultivate entrepreneurial thinking in your daily life, and how can creativity, resilience, and courage support you in overcoming challenges?
- How can focusing on the significance of your work, prioritizing service to others, lead to both personal fulfillment and business success?

Bio

Guest Expert - Dr. Randal Pinkett

Randal Pinkett, Ph.D., MBA, has established himself as an entrepreneur, speaker, author, and scholar. He is the co-founder, chairman, and CEO of BCT Partners, a global, multimillion-dollar research, training, consulting, technology, and data analytics firm. He is also an international public speaker, a regular contributor on MSNBC, CNN, and Fox Business News, and was the winner of NBC's hit reality television show, "The Apprentice." Additionally, he is the author or co-author of several books. Dr. Pinkett holds five engineering/computer science degrees and was the first and only African American to receive the prestigious Rhodes Scholarship at Rutgers University. He was inducted into the Academic All-America Hall of Fame as a former high jumper, long jumper, sprinter, and captain of the men's track and field team.

Conclusion

I trust you have found this book to be a treasure trove of valuable knowledge and expertise that will help you Sell More, Maximize Profit, and Finance Growth faster and easier. I appreciate the willingness of our high-achieving guest experts to share their knowledge freely within this book. You are welcome to reach out to connect with them via LinkedIn.

I also invite you to take advantage of Small Business Pro University's significant resources for helping you achieve greater business success faster and easier. You'll learn more about our proven Brain Trust Initiatives and expert advisory services to accelerate your growth. Further information is available on our website…

www.SBProU.com

Author Bio

Andrew Frazier, MBA, CFA
Masterpreneur and Founder
Small Business Pro University

Andrew Frazier, MBA, CFA, Masterpreneur™, and founder of Small Business Pro University, is revolutionizing how business owners scale. Through his groundbreaking Masterpreneur™ Journey Framework, Andrew helps entrepreneurs unlock their leadership potential and drive rapid, sustainable growth.

With over 15 years of experience as a business coach, consultant, and trainer, Andrew has worked 1-on-1 with over 1,000 business owners, identifying the key challenges that prevent them from reaching their goals. His Masterpreneur™ Journey Framework addresses critical knowledge gaps and skill deficiencies, offering a proven methodology that empowers business owners in any industry to lead confidently and achieve extraordinary results.

His unique, holistic approach combines business strategy, financial expertise, and leadership coaching to help entrepreneurs make data-driven decisions, optimize profits, and fuel sustainable growth. As an author of three influential business books, host of the "Leadership LIVE @ 8:05! Talking Small Business" Livestream/podcast with over 200 episodes, and organizer of high-impact business networking events over 12 years, Andrew's influence reaches tens of thousands of business owners, delivering actionable insights and multimillion-dollar results.

Andrew Frazier's journey from a paper route in 4th grade to a renowned business leader is a testament to his relentless drive and unmatched expertise. Andrew has developed a unique ability to guide business owners through complex challenges by combining his Engineering education at MIT, an MBA from NYU, and Chartered Financial Analyst (CFA) credentials with real-world experience as a naval officer, a Fortune 500 executive, and a serial entrepreneur. His diverse background allows him to bring a multifaceted perspective to every client, empowering them to achieve breakthrough results by evolving as leaders and transforming their businesses.

Business Tips

Revenue Generation Tips

Key Takeaways from Jimmy Newson:

- Start with a clear, actionable vision for your business.
- Focus on your most profitable, high-value products when exploring digital opportunities.
- Develop scalable digital assets that don't require your constant input.

Key Takeaways from Martha Krejci:

- Identify and write down business problem symptoms
- Research symptoms using Google
- Generate and refine content with AI Tools

Key Takeaways from Dr. Ravi R. Iyer:

- Gain control over your attention; it's the foundation of your reality.
- Learn to observe without rushing to apply, meaning open yourself to new possibilities.
- Once you create mental space, you unlock true freedom to grow and innovate.

Key Takeaways from Liz Heiman:

- Sales is problem-solving, not manipulation.
- Understand the financial math behind your sales process and investments.
- Manage your salespeople intentionally to set them up for success.

Key Takeaways from Barry Cohen:

- Highlight the benefits upfront, don't bury them; make them front and center.
- Always include a clear call to action in your messaging so people know exactly what you want them to do.
- Know and understand your audience and what is important to them.

Key Takeaways from Vedant Maheshwari:

- Take ownership of your brand's media and content, don't just rent attention.
- Build a robust short-form video content strategy to capture customer mindshare.
- Explore and implement AI tools now to stay ahead of the transformation curve.

Key Takeaways from Wallace Santos:

- Don't expect employees to automatically replicate your excellence; you must train them.
- Build processes and systems that help new hires understand what quality looks like.
- Create a culture of consistency, where everyone knows how to meet (and exceed) customer expectations.

Key Takeaways from Marc Williams:

- Practice and drill specific speaking skills.
- Seek out and learn from experts.
- Network and converse with a diverse range of people.

Key Takeaways from Sunil Bhaskaran:

- Start with a premium offer and build your process backward.
- Create discovery sessions that naturally lead into your offer.
- Build communities and systems that consistently fill your events and sessions with qualified leads.

Key Takeaways from Dale Favors:

- Listen carefully and continuously to customer needs.
- Stay flexible and ready to adapt your strategies and solutions.
- Build collaborative relationships to create greater value and new opportunities.

Key Takeaways from Stan Gibson:

- Develop deep self-awareness and lead authentically.
- Build strong, positive relationships that nurture your success and well-being.
- Invest in yourself consistently so you can better serve others.

Key Takeaways from Victor M. Nichols:

- Listening is your most valuable tool for building strong, aligned partnerships.
- Your credibility is built (or broken) by whether you keep your promises.
- Failure is part of the growth process. Stay resilient and keep innovating.

Key Takeaways from Stan Robinson:

- Always center your messaging around the problems you solve for your customers.
- Stay consistent with your visibility and engagement, even when results aren't immediately visible.
- Maintain a strong, professional LinkedIn presence and proactively focus your conversations on solving problems.

Key Takeaways from Precious L. Williams:

- Your external packaging influences the quality of opportunities you attract.
- Know how you are positioned and reposition if necessary to show up as elite.
- A compelling pitch makes you the obvious choice in a crowded marketplace.

Key Takeaways from Melinda Emerson:

- Start your business smartly by launching as a side hustle after careful research.
- Develop high-value content that speaks directly to your ideal customer's needs.
- Focus on retaining existing customers, who are more likely to buy again and spend more.

Profit Maximization Tips

Key Takeaways from Mel Solomon:

- The importance of the team: Success in business requires a strong, adaptable team.
- The necessity of a good strategy, having a clear strategy for product distribution and market penetration, is crucial.
- Embracing change, change should be at the center of business thinking.

Key Takeaways from Clevonne St. Hillaire:

- Believe in yourself fully and be willing to take strategic risks.
- Track every input and output to make smarter business decisions.
- Surround yourself with mentors and peers who push you to grow.

Key Takeaways from Doug C. Brown:

- Always focus on client acquisition, no matter what your business level.
- Know your ideal client, clearly identify your right-fit buyer to save time, energy, and money.
- Prioritize selling, especially when starting out; dedicate most of your efforts to sales activities to reach your first million dollars.

Key Takeaways from Gene Bohensky:

- Hire an assistant early to learn the art of delegation.
- List your daily and aspirational tasks to find what should be outsourced.
- Choose high-quality assistants through trustworthy sources for lasting success.

Key Takeaways from Josh Tan:

- Set dedicated time to measure business objectives and performance, rather than just planning to measure.
- Proactively plan to stop current problems and predict future issues before they arise.
- Foster team collaboration and accountability through regular meetings, encouraging open communication and shared responsibility.

Key Takeaways from Vanessa Zamy:

- Leverage leadership beyond financial considerations; focus on building and developing your team.
- Prioritize effective communication and active listening. Strong leadership requires effective communication, especially through active listening and asking thoughtful questions.
- Avoid hustle culture and prioritize well-being, recognize that stress is harmful and that hustle culture is unsustainable.

Key Takeaways from Jeneen Perkins:

- Organize and digitize your financial records to stay ready for tax season.
- Seek professional help immediately when you spot negative numbers.
- Prioritize strategic planning and budgeting, even when it feels difficult.

Key Takeaways from Paul Paray:

- Train your employees on good email hygiene to avoid cybersecurity threats.
- Protect your intellectual property early to safeguard your business's future value.
- Join associations and use free resources to stay informed and protected.

Key Takeaways from Perry Nunes:

- Track both your expenses and income consistently to stay financially clear.
- Use automation tools to simplify and streamline money management.
- Start with small financial systems and improve them over time.

Key Takeaways from Benjamin Dach:

- Keep organized and diligent notes on your ideas and when they were conceived.
- File your copyrights and patents early to ensure protection and prevent others from claiming your work.

- Don't hesitate to seek legal counsel and take advantage of pro bono services if necessary.

Key Takeaways from Julwel Kenney, Ph.D.:

- Build a financial safety net to cover at least six months of expenses.
- Obtain comprehensive insurance coverage, including health, disability, and workers' compensation.
- Carefully select a business partner who shares your values and vision.

Key Takeaways from Terry Trayvick:

- Repair and strengthen your core operations before seeking growth.
- Choose one clear growth strategy and commit to it.
- Decide what your business will compete on and strive to be the best at it.

Capital Acquisition Tips

Key Takeaways from Ervin Hughes Jr.:

- Establish and grow strong business credit to access larger contract opportunities.
- Expand into related goods and services within your industry for multiple revenue streams.
- Never use credit to pay bills; use credit to make money.

Key Takeaways from Richard Parker:

- Buying a business is achievable for everyday people, especially with tools like seller financing.
- Focus on the bigger goal and maintain a good relationship with the other party.
- Stay realistic about valuations, timelines, and expectations for a smooth deal.

Key Takeaways from Kevin Bibelhausen:

- Acquisition is a fast-track way to grow by adding complementary services without starting from scratch.
- Financing an acquisition is more accessible than many entrepreneurs realize, thanks to programs like SBA loans.
- A strong network and credible resources are essential to learning the right way to succeed.

Key Takeaways from Scott Springer:

- Establish a long-term strategy, develop a comprehensive strategy that includes growth targets and plans for building the desired company culture.
- Identify and address bottlenecks, continuously assess the business to identify key bottlenecks, whether in supply, equipment capacity, or personnel, and proactively develop plans to resolve them.
- Prioritize positive communication, ensure that leadership maintains constant, positive communication with all employees.

Key Takeaways from Calvin Reed:

- Create a comprehensive business plan. Having a solid business plan is crucial
- Utilize all available resources and seek information, don't hesitate to ask questions, and reach out to everyone in your network.
- Maintain determination and commitment, stay dedicated to the process.

Key Takeaways from Dr. Randall Pinkett:

- Discover your Ikigai, align passion, skill, need, and opportunity.
- Adopt entrepreneurial thinking, be creative, resilient, and courageous.
- Focus on significance, prioritize service to others over personal gain.

Guest Expert Books

Barry Cohen

- 10 Ways to Screw Up an Ad Campaign
- Startup Smarts: The Thinking Entrepreneur's Guide to Starting and Growing Your Business
- 10 Ways to Get Sued by Anyone and Everyone; The Small Business Owner's Guide to Staying Out of Court

Doug C. Brown

- Win-Win Selling: Unlocking Your Power for Profitability by Resolving Objections

Julwel Kenney

- Bringing Out the Best in You Through Life Challenges: It Is Your Time to Achieve
- How to Bring Out the Best in You: The Journal to Personal Transformation and Leadership
- Goals and Proven Strategies for Success By the Industry's Leading Experts

Martha Krejci

- The Home-Based Revolution: Create Multiple Income Streams from Home
- The Invincible Family Project: Everyday Families Creating Hope For Their Future

Melinda Emerson

- Become Your Own Boss in 12 Months: A Month-by-Month Guide to a Business that Works
- Become Your Own Boss in 12 Months, Revised and Expanded: A Month-by-Month Guide to a Business That Works Today!

Precious L. Williams

- Rainmaking 101 From Day 1 | Workbook
- The Pitch Queen: A Woman's Journey From Poverty To Purpose & Profits
- Pitching for Profit: The Bad Bitches' Playbook to Convert Conversations into Currency
- Bad Bitches and Power Pitches: For Women Entrepreneurs and Speakers
- Bad Bitches and Power Pitches | Workbook

Randal Pinkett

- Black Faces in High Places: 10 Strategic Actions for Black Professionals to Reach the Top and Stay There
- Data-Driven DEI: The Tools and Metrics You Need to Measure, Analyze, and Improve Diversity, Equity, and Inclusion
- Campus CEO: The Student Entrepreneur's Guide to Launching a Multi-Million-Dollar Business

Richard Parker

- How To Buy a Good Business at A Great Price

Scott Springer

- Manufacturing A Great Culture

Stan Gibson

- The Inspiration (Amazon Podcast)

Sunil Bhaskaran

- More Money, More Time, Less Stress: Laser Focus your Mind & Sky Rocket Your Results while Maintaining Balance
- The Forgiving Universe: A Path to Possibility

Vanessa Zamy

- FINISH: The Solopreneur's Guide to Getting Stuff Done

Victor Nichols

- VMN Business Talk (Amazon Podcast)

Websites

www.SmallBusinessLikeAPro.com

www.SBProU.com

Additional Websites
- **Courses** - https://learn.smallbusinessprouniversity.com/
- **Livestream and Podcast** – www.LiveAt805.com
- **Blog** - https://www.sbprou.com/sbpro-blog

Social Media

LinkedIn
- Personal Profile: AndrewFrazier
    - https://www.linkedin.com/in/andrewfrazier/
- Company Page:
    - https://www.linkedin.com/company/small-business-pro-university

Facebook
- Personal Profile: Andrew.Frazier.Jr
    - https://www.facebook.com/andrew.frazier.jr
- Company Page: SBProU
    - https://www.facebook.com/SBProU/

Twitter
- @Andrew_Frazier
    - https://twitter.com/Andrew_Frazier
- @SmBizLikeAPro
    - https://twitter.com/SmBizLikeAPro

Instagram
- SBProAF
    - https://www.instagram.com/SBProAF

YouTube
- Small Business Pro University
    - https://www.youtube.com/c/SmallBusinessProUniversity

Small Business Like A Pro

Helping entrepreneurs & small businesses owners to...

Grow Revenues
Increase Profitability
Obtain Financing

Providing entrepreneurs, business owners, and organizational leaders with access to the expertise, tools, and resources they need to compete effectively in this fast-paced, technology-driven, global business environment. Our services include:

- Coaching
- Consulting
- Training
- Speaking

www.RunningYourSmallBusinessLikeAPro.com

Small Business Pro University

Mission

Help 1,000,008 Entrepreneurs and Businesses Owners Grow Revenues, Increase Profitability, and Obtain Financing by 2028.

Vision

Become the leader in providing entrepreneurs, small business owners, and organizational leaders with access to the expertise, tools, and resources they need to compete effectively in this fast-paced, technology-driven, global business environment.

Values

Using Creativity to effectively combine Knowledge with Experience for entrepreneurs and small business owners to achieve Continual Improvement throughout their journey to develop a sustainable enterprise.

www.SBProU.com

Resources and Initiatives

Courses
- Individual Courses
- Bundled Courses

Training Programs
- Masterpreneur Training Program
- Masterpreneur Growth Accelerator

Coaching Programs
- 1-on-1
- SBPro Strategic
- Masterpreneur Playbook

SBPro University Press
- Books and Workbooks

Membership Groups
- Small Business Pro Network
- The Masterpreneur Club

Leadership LIVE @ 8:05 – Talking Small Business
- Livestream – Tuesdays @ 8pm EST
- Podcast – Thursdays @ 8am EST

Special Offer

Curated Collection of 250+ Livestream Episodes

Available to Members of the...

Join the Small Business Pro Network!

www.SBProNetwork.com

Stop Guessing. Start Growing.

Unlock the TRUE POTENTIAL of Your Business!

Get your personalized data-driven blueprint for scaling with confidence.

It only takes 10 minutes to change the way you grow your business.

Take the Assessment Now!

www.sbprou.com/take-the-assessment

www.ingramcontent.com/pod-product-compliance
Lightning Source LLC
Chambersburg PA
CBHW050140170426
43197CB00011B/1901